PI ANG

. PUBLIC EXPOSURE

She peered at the screen, as though she might just catch a glimpse of that someone, if she just looked carefully enough.

Time for a change of tactics, Lynda decided. Time to take the initiative with whoever was sitting at a computer out there somewhere linked to her. She willed him to answer.

"You're thinking about it, aren't you? *Aren't* you?"

She held her mystery writer for a moment longer and then lost contact. *MESSAGE ENDS* was the final cut-off.

Also available in Hippo Books:

PRESS GANG 1: First Edition

Cast list for
Press Gang

Lynda Day	JULIA SAWALHA
Spike Thomson	DEXTER FLETCHER
Kenny Phillips	LEE ROSS
Sarah Jackson	KELDA HOLMES
Colin Mathews	PAUL REYNOLDS
Frazz Davis	MMOLOKI CHRYSTIE
Julie Craig	LUCY BENJAMIN
Danny McColl	CHARLIE CREED-MILES
Tiddler	JOANNA DUKES
Matt Kerr	CLIVE WOOD
Chrissie Stuart	ANGELA BRUCE
Billy Homer	ANDY CROWE
Mr Homer	DUNCAN PRESTON
Jenny Eliot	SADIE FROST
Mr Sullivan	NICK STRINGER

Bill Moffat

PRESS GANG

3. PUBLIC EXPOSURE

Based on the original television series,
PRESS GANG
Scripts by Steven Moffat
Concept by Bill Moffat

Hippo Books
Scholastic Publications Limited
London

Scholastic Publications Ltd.,
10 Earlham Street, London WC2H 9RX, UK

Scholastic Inc.,
730 Broadway, New York, NY 10003, USA

Scholastic Tab Publications Ltd.,
123 Newkirk Road, Richmond Hill,
Ontario L4C 3G5, Canada

Ashton Scholastic Pty. Ltd.,
P O Box 579, Gosford, New South Wales,
Australia

Ashton Scholastic Ltd.,
165 Marua Road, Panmure, Auckland 6,
New Zealand

First published by Scholastic Publications Ltd, 1989

PRESS GANG – the book is based on the
original television scripts by Steven Moffat

Photographs reproduced by kind permission of
Central Independent Television plc and
Richmond Films & Television Ltd

ISBN 0 590 76163 3

Made and printed by
Cox & Wyman Ltd., Reading, Berks
Typeset in Times by AKM Associates (UK) Ltd.,
Southall, London

CONTENTS

Part One: INTERFACE

1.
MORNINGS

Mornings at the *Junior Gazette* had taken on a very established pattern and this one was no exception to that rule. Amid the usual bustle (though by any standards other than their own, it was a pretty *unusual* bustle) there were the familiar landmarks, the regular happenings. By twenty to eight, Fraser Davis, Frazz to his friends, was still asleep and Toni Tildesley, Tiddler to *her* friends, was distributing the mail. Holding out a fistful of letters, she confronted Editor Lynda Day – Lynda Day to *her* friends. "Mail?" Tiddler said, too chirpy for that time in the morning.

"No, female, since you ask," Lynda replied, taking the letters without breaking stride.

"Why are you always such a wise-guy in the mornings?" Tiddler was chirping in American now.

"Wise-gal, since you ask," was all that Tiddler was getting.

She went off on her post-round passing the still sleeping Frazz and depositing his letters in his open mouth – something which added a reedy quality to his snoring. Not an improvement. Lynda reached over and removed them without lifting her eyes from her own mail. It wasn't the first time she had had to rescue the letters in this way. It had become a sort of regular feature of her mornings. She would have to do something about it.

Over to Lynda's right a dejected Colin Mathews – the *Gazette*'s financial wizard – was sorting his quota of mail, dividing it between two waste bins, one marked "Bills" and the other "Final Demands". The latter ones he threw in with noticeably more venom! Life was not easy for Colin. He was the victim of mean and grasping people who kept asking him for money on the flimsy excuse that it was rightfully theirs! Why couldn't they be more charitable?

James Thomson, American, known to the whole world as Spike, and the genuine 24ct wise guy of the *Junior Gazette*, had fixed his attention on one pink envelope. He appeared to have fixed his nose to it as well. It was evidently perfumed – or at least that was what onlookers in general and Lynda in particular were meant to believe.

"Ah, the lovely Giselle," Spike murmured loudly enough for his particular audience to hear. He looked apologetically at Lynda, "I keep telling her never to write me at the office!"

Lynda raised a weary eyebrow. "Shall I tell you exactly how jealous that makes me?"

"Well if you're sure you've got the time . . ."

"OK. Listen." Lynda paused for a moment's silence and then, turning sharply on her heel, walked away.

Spike watched her go. He looked seriously impressed. "This must be good," he remarked to Tiddler. "She's going to take a run-up!"

There the repartee had to stop. Lynda was out of earshot and a breathless Colin was gibbering at his elbow.

"Spike! Look at this, just look at it! It came in the post."

Spike had little option. Colin had thrust the document directly in front of his eyes. Spike looked at it blankly.

"Wow!" His tone held little enthusiasm. "A photocopied page from a newspaper. Colin, you get all the best stuff."

But Colin would not be put off. "Look at the ringed advert!"

With line by line prompting from Colin, Spike grudgingly read the advert and discovered that there was a competition called "The Roxburgh Award for Creative Writing", with a first prize of an Amstrad Micro Computer and Printer. Not exactly earth shaking, Spike felt.

Colin was shaking, however, with excitement. "Don't you see?" he spluttered. "That's just what this office needs, Spike – a computer! Look at this place, it's *crawling* with writers! Real writers, talented writers, dedicated writers! These kids even *speak* in punctuation!"

Colin didn't usually express himself so enthusiastically when describing the talents of his colleagues – unless there was something in it for him; something material like money or goods.

None of it was making much sense to Spike. He tried to ask who had sent the clipping but Colin neither knew nor cared. It was obviously some well-wisher who had realized that it was a dead cert for the *Junior Gazette* to produce the winner. It was a gift horse and oral examinations were out! Spike shook his head, mystified, and returned the clipping to Colin, firmly reminding him to let Lynda know.

Such warnings were needless, Colin assured him – and went on assuring him. "I wouldn't dream of *not* telling Lynda! No, no, no!" As he retreated to his desk Colin's tone became quite hurt. "As if I'd go using Lynda's news team without asking her permission."

The following morning strayed from the established pattern. Frazz was still sleeping and Tiddler was still on the mail round – she had stuck the letters in the V-neck of his sweater this time and Lynda had removed them on her arrival at her desk – but Colin was *not* disposing of his bills. Instead he was in the concluding stages of a meeting with the news team.

"OK, you lot, let's fight it out like gentlemen." Lynda was suddenly aware of the meeting, as Colin pressed on. "We all know there can only be one winner so let's forget all those dirty tricks, let's forget about cutting the difficult words out of the spelling dictionary . . . And people – let's just keep the strong language on the page, shall we?"

Lynda was puzzled, growing interested and getting angry in that order. She closed in on

Colin. Could they have a word? Her tone was ominously restrained.

It was not the right moment with Colin in full cry and revving up to his climax. "With you in a moment, Lynda," he slipped in, while exhorting the news team to greater effort. "Right kids, we want a good, clean write. So let's just get out there and do some fiction."

It all had the desired effect. The team ran off with suitable "Whoops" and "Yeahs", like an American football team after a pep talk. It had the desired effect on all but Lynda, that is.

"Just what are you doing, Colin?" she snapped.

Colin was ready for her, and hyped up, and smug – a pretty bad combination. With a self-satisfied smile, he handed over the clipping.

Lynda looked at the photocopy briefly. " 'The Roxburgh Award'? Never heard of it." She was not pleased.

Colin, on the other hand, was pleased enough for both of them. "But you have heard of computers," he said, wagging his head and smiling patiently as though she were a naughty child. Then a quick change of gear and enthusiastic once more: "I could do great things with a computer, Lynda. Our accounts, our bills, everything."

"Really?" Lynda was exasperated. She waved her hand at the departing writers. "And what am I supposed to do – without a news team?"

"Oh, that's typical, isn't it! How can you always justify putting your own personal, petty little desires before mine?"

Lynda had had enough. She had more to do

than become tangled up in whatever it was that Colin did instead of thinking.

At least all was clearer now. Colin had found a way that someone could win a prize for him. "For the *Gazette*," he had said, but to Colin the *Gazette* was a front for Colin Mathews Enterprises! Material gain was the motive, and that at least was reassuring.

A fortnight later at about the same time, a similar bustle was in progress, though on this occasion it was from between Frazz's feet that Lynda retrieved his mail and dropped the letters on his desk. Lynda was definitely of the opinion that someone else should take over this particular duty.

"Remind me to get someone else for letter duty, Frazz," she said.

But Frazz neither heard nor said a word. He slept on peacefully.

"And remind me to get someone else to remind me," she added, ruefully.

From behind her a voice, gleefully and unmistakably Colin's, proclaimed, "We're on the home straight!"

A startled Lynda only managed a startled, "What!?"

"The competition – Sarah's on the short list."

Lynda was incredulous. "They published the short list before the closing date?"

"It's unofficial. This is inside information. Lynda, I can almost taste that computer – in megabytes."

"We haven't got it yet, Colin!"

"Maybe not," Colin conceded. "But this is the clincher!" He handed her some stapled sheets.

Lynda read aloud. " 'The Early Life of Sarah Jackson'. You're sending *this*?"

Her voice would have risen in disbelief had it not already been pitched at squeak level.

But Colin was unstoppable. "I'm going for the sympathy angle. All her early hardships, that sort of stuff. There'll be tears in their eyes when they tell her she's won."

"What early hardships?"

"Hey, if any of this were true it wouldn't be clever," Colin protested.

Lynda was reading aloud again, or rather squeaking aloud. " 'Alcoholic parents' 'No formal education' '. . . only recently learned *English*'. Colin, *no*!"

"OK, I'll tone it down a bit. But if we lose because we're playing fair, you're going to feel so guilty!" And he meant every word.

Three weeks later there was the usual unusual morning bustle – except that Frazz was awake, well more or less awake. Between yawns he managed to catch Tiddler's attention.

"OK Tiddler, where did you put my letters?" He did not manage to get a reply.

Nor was Lynda carrying out her usual duty, though she hadn't yet succeeded in unloading it on to anyone else either. This time the letters were protruding from the back of Frazz's trousers and Lynda accurately but unhelpfully told him, "Behind you."

Frazz swung round and continued to look

mystified. "Where?"

"Behind you!"

He swung again, demanded again and was about to be told again, when Lynda's eye caught something else.

The news team were gathered around Colin's desk, which was not a good sign. Lynda made her way across the room. The cause of the interest was clear. There on Colin's desk lay the brand new Amstrad PC complete with printer and modem. And hovering above the computer was the beaming face of Colin himself.

"Well?" he said, and there was a wealth of invitation in that one syllable.

Lynda was impressed. "Sarah, well *done*! But no big deal or anything? No presentation ceremony?" Lynda was puzzled.

"Next month, some time," Sarah replied. "But it won't be me that's at it."

Spike reached past the confused Lynda and lifted the letter which lay on top of the new machine.

He read out, ". . . the Roxburgh Award this year goes to Colin Mathews for his moving story – 'The Early Years of Sarah Jackson'."

Colin continued the explanation. "I *sent* it as a letter. They thought it was fiction!"

Which, Sarah pointed out, was most certainly so!

Lynda shook her head. She felt she had never really caught up with this particular escapade, but all's well that end's well . . . she decided a little uncertainly, and shrugged. The question half formed in her mind was – "Had it ended yet?"

Aloud she said, "Well, anyway – well done, both of you." And added for good measure, "Well done everyone." She turned her attention back to the computer for a moment, and continued, "And I'll catch up with the new baby later, all right?" Then more briskly, "Kenny – business!"

Kenny Phillips was Lynda's assistant and right hand everything. The two were soon deep in discussion about an editorial problem, something that Matt Kerr, Editor of the senior paper had drawn to their attention. Anything from that source had to be dealt with seriously and urgently.

Yet there was something about that Roxburgh Award business. Lynda's mind wandered off their discussion. She looked back at the computer.

"You know, Kenny . . . somehow that all seemed just too easy."

Kenny didn't follow her drift. And Lynda, apart from frowning and shaking her head in a troubled way, didn't offer any explanation. They resumed their discussion.

2.
LINK UP

It hadn't taken too long to set up the computer and run some of the basic programmes which came with it. The word processor was straightforward enough, though for the really clever tricks they'd have to study the manual. The same thing applied to the spreadsheet and the database.

Colin was fascinated. With the spreadsheet he could perform all manner of minor miracles – and, more importantly, make a profit. He was energetically explaining to some of the news team how a change in price or quantity of any item was immediately taken into account and a new costing produced. For Colin there was true beauty in that. An impatient Julie Craig, Graphics and Design, was desperate to get her hands on the graphics package. Already she could see a whole new world of possibilities.

Lynda saw the machine as a means of communication, and that afternoon they were ready to try out the link-up with Norbridge High, the school most of them attended. The modem, which had come with the computer, transmitted and received data downline through the phone, and now the first trial of the system was under way.

In the school Danny McColl, Staff Photographer on the *Gazette* team, sat in front of a computer console. He was speaking on the phone to Lynda, back at the newsroom. He confirmed that he was ready and set the modem at his end ready for use. Preparations were completed at the newsroom too. Lynda crossed her fingers and breathed rather than spoke the words, "OK. Here goes!"

Danny, in the school, echoed Lynda's tension with his own "Here goes!" Watched by school secretary, Miss Hessope, he struck the first key. Anxious eyes in the newsroom watched the blank screen for what seemed an age. Suddenly, and marked by a sharp intake of collective breath, the words *MESSAGE BEING RECEIVED* flowed, letter by letter, across the screen. A pause and then came *THIS IS A SMALL STEP FOR MANKIND BUT IT IS A BIG ONE FOR THE JUNIOR GAZETTE*! Another pause and *MESSAGE ENDS*. It was greeted with a cheer from just about everybody plus an excited verdict from Lynda.

"We've got it. We've got the whole thing!"

Kenny and Sarah were standing apart from the rest talking intently about the winning of the computer rather than the working of it. Sarah was having no more success than Lynda had at persuading Kenny that there was anything odd in it.

"Because it's strange, that's why," she persisted. "Roxburgh are an office supplies firm. What have they got to do with creative writing? And if it's just for the publicity, where is the *publicity*? I haven't seen any! Kenny, there is something weird about this."

Kenny was not to be moved. "Like you not winning?" he asked, perhaps unfairly.

Sarah ignored the remark. "And look at the prize. First it's a computer and printer. Then there's a modem phone link thrown in as well."

"What's wrong with that? It's going to be really useful for us."

"It's perfect for us, Kenny! It's too good to be true!"

Kenny shrugged. Sarah persisted. "I want to do an interview. Find out a bit more. The Roxburgh head office is just in the High Street – and they've just given us a computer. What could be more natural?"

"OK. So long as it really is an interview and not just you proving some little theory of yours."

Sarah grinned. "You mean there is a difference?"

As they spoke, another message came through on the screen. It said, *DID IT WORK*?

Lynda replied by typing the one word, *PERFECTLY*.

At the other end Danny jumped up and down and shouted, "It works! Miss Hessope, it works!"

And that wasn't the last message of the series. Lynda found herself confronted with the statement, *WE NOW HAVE THE COMPUTER DATING AGENCY ON LINE.*

"What's this supposed to be?" she hissed. "Is someone having a joke?"

As though in reply the message continued, *LYNDA DAY*?

It blinked at her until at last Lynda responded by typing in *YES*.

YOUR PERFECT PARTNER, the computer now proclaimed, *IS SPIKE THOMSON*!

Everyone was amused. Everyone, that is, but Lynda. As the realization dawned, she spat out her "perfect partner's" name, while away at the other end of the line Spike was laughing and saying to Danny, "I wish I could see her face." He would not have been disappointed.

The computer had stolen the show for the day and it was left on when the team left the newsroom that evening. Lynda was anxious about the possibility that someone might try to contact them. Perhaps it was that uneasy feeling both she and Sarah had experienced about the whole business of the competition. In a crazy way it reminded her of a science fiction thing she had once seen on TV, an old black and white programme. Plans for a kind of radio receiver mysteriously came into the hands of a scientist. He constructed it and discovered that he had enabled aliens from another planet to transport themselves to earth, with not very friendly intentions. What had seemed a gift, a kind of prize for being the one scientist clever enough to understand the instructions, turned out to be a trick. Lynda wasn't expecting any little green men to appear in the newsroom, yet . . . yet that computer had come into their lives in the same flattering sort of way. Winners of a competition which no one had heard of, except them. Some publicity stunt!

Kenny, however, resolutely refused to share her apprehension. He would have been both amazed and doubly disbelieving if he had had the faintest suspicion that Lynda Day, of all people, entertained such fantasies, dredged up from some half-remembered relic of a TV series! Not Lynda.

"Who's got a computer and modem that's going to be sending us messages tonight?" he asked, and didn't expect an answer.

But Lynda, true to form, had the answer and it was not one that he particularly wanted to hear. "Your dad's got the equipment – and you still haven't given me that article on homework, have you?"

"Hey! Great art doesn't happen overnight," Kenny replied.

Lynda smiled a little too sweetly. She turned back to the computer and patting it, said, "Now it can."

It was twenty past ten and both of them were tired. As they pushed the swing doors of the newsroom open, Kenny asked, "Don't you ever get sick of this place?"

It was a silly question. Lynda answered with a simple "No," and snapped off the lights. At that moment, unheard by either of them, a faint beep from the computer intimated that someone with the right equipment was getting in touch. Letter by letter, *MESSAGE BEING RECEIVED*, flickered across the screen, and there, unseen in the darkened newsroom, the mystery had begun.

3.

THE MYSTERY WRITER

It was morning again in the newsroom. From this day forth the abbreviation "a.m." took on a new meaning – after micro. The paper was now partially computerized. Apart from that, everything was much as would be expected. Sarah was on the phone to her mother explaining her intention to be late home from school.

"Just a little later, Mum, just a little later after school than normal . . . No, it's not because of your cooking, Mum. I'm doing an interview . . . I *loved* last night's dinner, really . . . Look, Dad called it a burnt offering as a *compliment*. He meant it was like a religious experience." Her creativity outstripped her diplomacy, but all was fair at the *Junior Gazette* in the morning!

As in all other mornings Frazz and Tiddler were duelling over the mail. This time Frazz had the advantage of being awake – but he was faring no better than usual. In desperation he resorted to a surrender and a straightforward whine from the heart.

"OK, Tiddler, where are they? Where are my letters?"

Finally, Tiddler took silent pity on the sleep-confused Frazz and wordlessly answered his plea by plucking at the middle of his sweater. The letters fluttered down on to Frazz's feet.

Despite appearances to the contrary, Lynda still hadn't given up the duty of mail retriever for Frazz. Kenny had waylaid her earlier and presented her with a printout from the computer. "It came in on the computer last night," Kenny commented. "Remember that television review column you wanted? I think this could be it."

"It's excellent," Lynda agreed. "But short. We'd need about the same again."

Kenny ignored Lynda's judgment. He was more interested in the way the material had arrived. "The weird thing is – it's anonymous."

Despite Lynda's science fiction fantasies of the previous night, she was all matter-of-fact now – now that it suited her. "It'll be one of the news team. They'll just have forgotten to put their name on it, that's all!"

Kenny was far from convinced. "Are there a lot on the news team who forget their names?"

But Lynda was not in the mood for mysteries. "Just find out who it was and get them to double the length."

"And I don't recognize the style – do you?" Kenny continued.

"Don't make a mystery of it, Kenny."

"And who's got a computer with a modem

anyway?" Kenny called after Lynda, now making her way down the newsroom believing the matter to be settled.

"Kenny!" The single name was delivered with a mixture of warning and finality that convinced Kenny, at least for the moment.

The little Amstrad PC was managing to attract quite an aura of mystery around it – how it arrived and, now, what it was displaying on its screen. Sarah was determined to investigate the Roxburgh Award Scheme and see what light that would shed. At least she would, if she could just find a way of getting off the phone, and time was not on her side. She planned a visit to the firm's headquarters on her way home from school if she could just persuade her mother that this was not part of a family conspiracy to avoid dinner. Finally, with much reassuring and more tact, she disengaged successfully.

After what had seemed an interminable day at school, Sarah finally arrived at Roxburgh's. She was immediately shown into the General Manager's Office. Mr Douglas Homer was seated behind his desk and rose to greet Sarah as she entered. He was a big man with a friendly face which broke into a welcoming smile as they shook hands. He invited her to be seated.

The room was much as she had expected. Not a showplace, but a workplace. It suited the man, who looked a capable and energetic individual, at home in his world and very much in charge of himself as well as his firm. On the wall behind the desk and occupying pride of place, was the framed poster of the Roxburgh Award. It was probably the only thing in the room that didn't have a practical use.

"And how can I help you, young lady?" he enquired encouragingly.

Sarah found it easy to speak to him. She asked a few opening questions about the firm and its background before closing in on the mysterious award.

"Were there many entries? Was the standard high? What in particular did the judges look for?"

Mr Homer was quick and to the point in his answers. Yet, for all that, he seemed not to provide much information. Sarah felt there was a lack of detail and, as she struggled to pin him down, she felt he might even be toying with her. She decided to go for a more direct approach.

"Mr Homer, why would an office supplies firm take such an interest in creative writing?"

If Douglas Homer noticed the accusation in Sarah's tone, he showed no sign of it. Instead he patiently explained why it was perfectly natural for a company such as his to be enthusiastic about the written word.

"D'you know what office supplies are about?" he asked, and went straight on to answer his own question. "Words! Making words, storing words, sending words, recording words. Without words we're nothing. So what better than a creative writing competition?"

Sarah was taken off guard by the energy and enthusiasm in his voice – or was it that he protested too much? Certainly she had struck some kind of nerve. It was time for the trump card.

"How about publicity? I didn't see much. In fact I didn't see any except for a photocopied advert sent to our office." The accusation in Sarah's voice was now transparent.

The manager studied her for a moment, his face serious. Then he smiled.

"Do you know how much publicity we had, Miss Jackson?"

Sarah was interested. It showed in her expression.

"Enough," Douglas Homer concluded, and then, looking meaningfully at his watch, added, "now if you don't mind . . ."

The interview was at an end and the Manager rose to show Sarah out. Sarah returned his smile and replied, "Not at all, Mr Homer. I've got all I need."

Softening the rather abrupt end to their meeting Douglas Homer said, "I hope it wasn't too boring for you. Did you come straight from school?"

"Yes," Sarah smiled, and nodded. Then, as an afterthought, she turned in the doorway and commented, "That's the trouble with school – it always gets in the way of work."

Douglas Homer laughed as he closed the door behind her. He shook his head ruefully as he eyed the overfilled intray on his desk and reflected that Miss Jackson would find out soon enough that work gets in the way of work!

Sarah had only gone halfway down the corridor when she suddenly remembered something.

"My bag!" she blurted out, and turned to make her embarrassed way back, smiling and explaining as she passed Mr Homer's secretary, who returned her smile and nodded to go right in.

Sarah tapped on the door and stuck her head tentatively round, saying as she did so, "Sorry, Mr Homer, I forgot my . . ." She tailed off at what she saw and hesitated for a few telltale seconds before finishing weakly, "bag."

Mr Homer was caught in the act. He was removing the Roxburgh Award poster from its place on the wall, and it wasn't only in Sarah's overworked imagination that Douglas Homer looked guilty. Or, at least, Sarah had lost any doubts she may have had, by the time she had returned to the newsroom.

"You'd have thought it had only been up there for my benefit," she told Lynda. "Weird, isn't it?"

But Lynda was not really listening. "Kind of, I suppose," she said, absently. Then she picked up the computer print-out which Kenny had given her earlier. "Speaking of weird," she continued and offered the paper to Sarah, "I've asked everyone else – did *you* write this?"

Sarah took the print-out and studied it for a moment. "No. Why?"

"It came through on the computer. Someone on the news team's gone anonymous . . ." Lynda directed the rest of her remarks to the whole team who had by now gathered round ". . . and I am not happy about it!" Holding up the paper, she went on, "Now this is *good.* It's snappy, it's witty – if it can be brought up to length it's going in. But not without a name. And the name belongs to someone sitting at this table." She fixed each member of the team in turn with a probing look. There were no takers.

"And in case anyone thinks I'm jumping to conclusions, think about this. Who knows we've got a computer with a modem link *and* knows how to write this stuff *and* knows I was looking for a television column in the first place? Only the people I am looking at right now."

Still no takers.

Lynda pressed on. "It's as simple as this. I want the review doubled in length, and I want the name of the writer."

The uncomfortable silence was broken by Spike. "Lynda, you'd better get over here!" His voice had that singsong quality which meant that he knew something that she didn't.

Lynda's reply was irritable. "Spike, this is a meeting."

The singsong continued: "It's your friend again!"

"*What*?" But Lynda wasn't waiting for a reply. She dived over to the computer in time to see the words scrolling up-screen, under the heading – *TV REVIEW – EXPANDED VERSION*.

"Well, that's neat!" It was Kenny who pronounced the verdict. With an all-embracing wave of the hand he declared, "That eliminates everyone on the paper."

Lynda was bewildered. "Who's doing this? Who could?" She was asking herself more than anything, thinking aloud.

Nevertheless Kenny felt impelled to respond. "More to the point, do we use it? We've only got two hours to make up our minds."

Lynda finished reading. "Kenny, it's too

good not to."

"But who do we say wrote it?" Kenny reminded her.

The answer to that particular question came not from Lynda but from Colin. Lynda was ready for Matt Kerr when she took the news of their intention to run the anonymous TV column.

"Making a virtue out of a necessity," she told the Senior Editor. "It was Colin's idea when I told him we didn't have a name. If you haven't got it, flaunt it. He runs his business enterprises on that same philosophy. Though he did suggest Mr E Writer. Clever, but obscuring it instead of flaunting it."

"Rather depends on your readership, does it not?" Matt Kerr replied with a grin. "Depends whether they read out loud – then it would work! But I think you're right. Flaunting obscurely is perhaps not the best plan. So! You are now getting mysterious messages on the computer you mysteriously won in a competition whose publicity can only be described as mysterious."

Lynda smiled weakly. She felt that Mr Kerr was perhaps not taking her too seriously. She rallied and replied, "Yes. Mysterious, isn't it?"

Outside Matt Kerr's office Chrissie Stuart, Assistant Editor of the big paper, leaned against the wall, hugging her clipboard. Chrissie had the unenviable task of keeping an eye on the fledgling *Junior Gazette* and she took any opportunity to catch a word with Lynda, particularly after the Junior Editor had been to see her senior counterpart.

"So how did it go down?" she asked Lynda as

she emerged from Matt Kerr's office.

"It sunk – at first, anyway. I think he'll live with it."

Chrissie nodded. What else could you expect from "that man"? It was a silent comment. Out loud she said, "Tell me honestly, Lynda. Is it a gimmick? Or do you really not know who it is?"

Lynda couldn't believe what she was hearing. The whole thing had cost her too much sleep, and now Chrissie was suggesting that it was just some cheap trick to boost circulation. "A *gimmick*?" Lynda repeated. "To sell papers, you mean?"

"If it is, it could be a good one."

Lynda wasn't having any. "What kind of person would invent a situation like this just to sell papers?" Lynda turned on her heel and left.

4.
MOZART AND FRIENDS

But not everyone saw the mystery situation in the same light as Lynda. In the Norbridge High playground, Colin Mathews, arch flaunter of what he didn't have, stood on a box, a bundle of *Junior Gazettes* wedged under his arm. Behind him, the school doors were adorned with "MYSTERY SPECIAL" posters for the *Junior Gazette* showing the outline of a face with only a question mark where there should have been features. In huge letters the posters asked, "WHO IS THE MYSTERY WRITER?" and commanded, "BUY THE JUNIOR GAZETTE!" A host of the junior school had gathered around and were held under the spell of the sales pitch.

Colin was in great form. "Who *is* the Mystery Writer? Are rumours of a royal connection true? Only *you* can decide with a competitively priced copy of the *Junior Mystery Gazette*. Can *you* see through the mask to the mysterious face beyond?"

He fixed some of the smallest and most gullible of his audience with a beady and accusing stare. "Get your copy now while it's still a mystery!"

They obediently searched their pockets for cash and gradually formed into a queue. Sales were brisk.

From a distance away the scene was watched by a disbelieving Lynda standing alongside Kenny. She said, "Does this make your skin crawl?"

Kenny looked mildly surprised. "Come on, Lynda, look what it's doing for publicity. We're really selling this week."

"*Et tu, Brute*," Lynda thought. Then aloud, she replied, "Yeah. Our souls." It was more sigh than sentence.

Lynda wanted the mystery TV Reviews because they were well written. Well written copy sold newspapers. Colin saw public interest in a good mystery (properly exploited). An interested public bought newspapers. What was the difference? Whatever the ethics of Colin's ceaseless enterprise and exploitation of their mystery, it could not be denied that circulation was at record levels. Kenny thought better of explaining all this to the troubled Lynda. Instead he nodded and smiled rather vaguely.

Things were no better back at the newsroom and the problems there were doing nothing for circulation – in fact they had no saving grace. Lynda sat back in her chair and watched the mad mad world that her newsroom had become. Actually she blamed herself. She should never have put the advert in. What would you expect if you invite a mystery writer to unmask herself/himself? A queue of cranks. That's exactly what you'd expect – just like the one that had now formed along the back wall.

Lynda looked at them. A mixed crew of oddballs – an unsavoury bunch by any standards. She looked at them again. The idea of those characters writing those snappy little gems that came downline on to the computer was a non-starter. It was all too silly. Why did she ever start it with that stupid advert? She couldn't even think of somebody to blame.

Lynda was working her way along the queue assessing each in turn when her attention was diverted by a rap at the door. Another entrant – in fancy dress! She watched Danny McColl admit a pink-haired punk with a spectacular Mohican and complete with a leather jacket festooned with chains which jangled as he moved.

"It's me!" the pink punk announced.

"What?" Danny enquired.

"I'm the Mystery . . ." he started, but did not finish. The word had escaped him.

The guy was no Einstein, Danny reckoned. "Writer?" he prompted.

"Yeah! I knew it was a big word."

"In you come. Far wall, join the queue."

This one was even more unlikely than the curly-haired affair second from the front, if that was possible. Lynda allowed her attention to transfer now to the candidate being questioned by Kenny. She was a little old lady, with a striking resemblance to Miss Marple. Lynda picked up the exchange.

". . . and I saw your advert asking for any information about the Mystery Writer, so I thought I'd better come forward," little old Miss Marple was saying.

"So it's you, is it?" Kenny enquired patiently.

She laughed. "Oh it's not *me*, oh no. I am simply the medium through which he has communicated from the other side."

"The other side? He's dead?"

"He has passed over."

Kenny was intrigued and exasperated in equal measure. "Anyone we know?"

Your Mystery Writer is none other than Wolfgang Amadeus Mozart!"

Kenny turned to Lynda. "What did I tell you? Mozart!"

"I've got to get some fresh air," Lynda said, wearily.

On her way, Lynda was confronted by Sarah. "I've got a theory about the Mystery Writer!"

It was about the last thing Lynda had wanted to hear just at that moment. "Another one?" she retorted wearily. "I've had three weeks of this, Sarah. I've listened to so many theories, I'm twitching!"

As Lynda disappeared through the swing doors, Sarah called after her, "But this is a good one!"

The slam of the outside door was all the reply that Sarah was going to get for the time being. Outside Lynda slumped against the wall, eyes closed and inhaling gently – calming her shattered nerves. Alone at last – if you didn't count Colin! She couldn't believe it. It had to be a conspiracy.

There was Colin large as life and at his shiftiest, peering round the corner of the building. He stepped into full view and announced, "I was just on my way in to see you. He's here."

"Who?"

As she spoke, Lynda slumped and closed her eyes again. Something was telling her that she should not have asked that question. "The Mystery Writer?"

"Who else?"

Lynda thought. Was there anyone in town who *wasn't* the Mystery Writer?

"Round you come!" Colin was speaking to an unseen figure around the corner.

Lynda opened one eye to see a hooded figure all in black appear behind the building.

So the Mystery Writer doubles as the local hangman. Well, she could use a hangman just about now, she decided.

Colin was speaking again. "This is Lynda Day, the Editor. Lynda, this is the man himself – the Mystery Writer!"

The hooded figure bowed solemnly. Lynda smiled bleakly in return.

"Let me guess," she said. "He wants to be paid and you're here to handle the finances."

"I told you she would understand," Colin reassured the hooded figure.

"You bet I understand!" The words were fired rather than spoken, and Lynda whipped the hood off. "Do *you* understand, Frazz?"

The Mystery Hangman was now a sheep, or at least giving an excellent imitation of one!

Colin, on the other hand, was giving a very bad

imitation of being surprised. "My God, Lynda, it's Frazz! He must have been trying to trick us. Frazz, how could you *do* this?"

Lynda was not convinced. "Colin! Find another country – pronto!" There was no imitation here.

Colin continued his assault on Frazz. "You see how upset you've made her, Frazz? She doesn't know what she's saying!"

For the third time Lynda slumped and closed her eyes. It was all despair.

5.
NIGHTCALLERS

The whole mystery writer thing was preying on Lynda's mind. Increasingly she found herself locked in solitary conversation with the computer. That night, after deporting Colin to any other country, after everyone else had gone home, she sat in front of the glowing screen. On time the TV review had come downline, just as good as every other time. Elbows on the desk, chin set in cupped hands, Lynda stared at the screen.

"Do you know something, Mystery Writer?" Lynda said. "You're ruining my life. I'm surrounded by people who only ever talk about you – who you are, why you're doing this, whether or not you're Mozart. But I'll say one thing for you – I can talk to you. Oh, I mean it's not much of relationship. I mean all you ever do is write television reviews at me. But I'll tell you this – you're the sanest person around here at the moment."

Lynda leaned closer to the screen. "That you finished for the night, is it? Another witty little masterpiece?"

She didn't really expect an answer. She was used to these one-sided chats. She leaned back in her chair and stretched, her mind already set on going home. Suddenly there were letters appearing on the screen. They spelled out: *HELLO*. Not so one-sided after all. This was unexpected and Lynda was not sure what she was meant to do. Tentatively she typed in the obvious reply. *HELLO*.

Mystery man was talkative tonight. *NAME?* now appeared on the screen and Lynda obliged by typing *LYNDA DAY*.

I SAW YOUR ADVERT. The computer informed her, or rather someone informed her through the computer.

She peered at the screen, as though she might just catch a glimpse of that someone, if she looked carefully enough.

Time for a change of tactics, Lynda decided. Time to take the initiative. She typed *NAME*? and waited. Nothing. She could almost feel the contact with whoever was sitting at a computer out there somewhere linked to her. She willed him to answer.

"You're thinking about it, aren't you? *Aren't* you?"

She held her mystery writer for a moment longer and then lost contact.

MESSAGE ENDS was the final cut-off.

But Lynda had the last word. "Damn!" she said, and banged her fist on the desk.

These little conversations had become a regular evening feature – not every night but often enough. Lynda tried every time to extract her caller's name, or even a clue, but the moment she went off on that tack, it was always – *MESSAGE ENDS*.

As she left the newsroom after the fourth or fifth of the unhelpful interludes she happened to notice that the light in Matt Kerr's office was still on. She tapped on the door and put her head round.

"Can I have a word, Mr Kerr?"

He nodded without lifting his eyes from the papers on his desk. A brief gesture with his hand invited Lynda to take a seat. Over the months, she had become more used to speaking to this rather intimidating man, but she was never entirely at her ease, she was always conscious of a sense of intruding. As she sat there she remembered the first time. It all seemed so long ago. So much had happened since she had first found herself Editor of a newspaper whose entire stafff seemed to be appointed because they had been falling short of what was expected of them elsewhere – mainly at Norbridge High. Appointment by default. There were a few who had volunteered, or at least thought they had volunteered. One way or another they had all landed there because it was going to be good for them. Right now it wasn't good for Lynda.

She hadn't long to wait before she had his attention. Her thoughts were interrupted by Matt Kerr's voice. "That's one of the great privileges of rank, Lynda," he said. "Here we are, Editors of our papers, both allowed to work later than anyone else." He paused and smiled. "How can I help you? Let me guess. It's about your Mystery Writer, I imagine."

Lynda smiled. "Right first time, but no prize. It didn't take Sherlock Holmes to figure that out."

"No, I suppose not, but I gather you're in need of a spot of detection. What's he, or she, been up to this time?"

"Talking to me. Asking my name. Telling me things but not the things *I* want to know."

"How often has this happened?"

"A few times – all recently. It's the same pattern always. The moment I get close to asking for a name – Goodbye!"

Matt Kerr thought for a moment. "But in a way, he – or she – invites the question?" It was as much statement as question.

Lynda nodded. "I just don't understand it. Who could be doing this?"

Someone who's trying very hard to hide from you . . . and who's very frightened that they might succeed."

"You mean whoever it is *wants* to be found?"

"Are there ever any clues left for you? Any hints?"

"No."

"Funny. It doesn't fit the psychology for there to be no clues." Matt Kerr glanced down at his watch. "Anyway, Lynda . . ."

"Can't we talk a bit more?"

"Lynda . . ." Matt Kerr was gentle but insistent.

"I know you're busy. But there's no one else I can talk to. Everyone at the office has gone mad on this thing." Lynda tailed off as a thought struck her. "Well . . . almost everyone . . ."

There would just be time, but none to waste. Lynda jumped to her feet. "Thank you Mr Kerr," she said hurriedly. "You've been a great help." And she meant it. She rushed back to her own desk and checked through the small index of addresses to confirm she had the right one. Then she was out the door and on her way.

The whole thing was too important to bother about formalities, otherwise she would certainly have had some doubts about the wisdom of what she was doing. At last she found the house.

Typical, Lynda thought – no number and no name. She double-checked just to make sure she had the right door, and rang the bell. She gave it all of three seconds, and then started to mutter under her breath, "Come on. *Come* on." The door was opened by a tall, slimly-built man to whom Lynda rushed out her reason for calling, with all her impatient urgency.

He grinned. "You'll find him up there," he said. "First on the left."

The door was open and Lynda could hear the TV set and a familiar voice joining in with the film. She paused to listen.

"Come on, it's the guy with the beard. How many times has this been on and you still don't know *that*?!" Now it was all sarcastic. "Oh, that's right, let her go down the corridor on her own, she's sure to be safe there!" Now it became reflective. "I should get a part in this film, I know it backwards."

Lynda stepped forward into the doorway and

saw the owner of the voice prone on his bed watching television. He sensed her presence and without turning round said, "Hi, Dad. It's that film again. The plate's over there."

Lynda's eyes followed the direction indicated by the pointing thumb to see a food-crusted plate on a table close to where she stood. She did nothing to dispel the notion that it was his dad who had arrived.

The commentary on the film resumed. "Can't you tell he's looking shifty? Look at him! You should have read the script." Then it was back to Dad again. "Oh, Dad, I need some clean underwear and it's your turn to do the washing. There's a bag of dirty stuff on the chair."

Throughout the conversation the eyes never left the screen. He simply reached over, lifted the bag and handed it absently over his shoulder.

Lynda looked at the rather unprepossessing bundle now on offer to her, and then said in a clear voice, most definitely not his father's, "I can't tell how much this means to me, Spike!"

The figure on the bed convulsed, performed something approaching one and a half somersaults with full twist while emitting a kind of yelp. Before hitting the floor Spike had also managed to scoop up several personal items which he drop-kicked under the bed as he landed.

To Lynda he said, in a strangled tone, "So – ah . . . Fancy meeting you here." And then with growing composure, "And I do."

Lynda said, "I want to talk, Spike."

"OK, let's talk Spike," Spike replied, executing an acrobatic return to his bed and launching into his autobiography. "Well, I was born in New York, just the two parents but there was one of each . . ."

"About the Mystery Writer," Lynda interjected, firmly.

"OK, let's talk about the Mystery Writer."

"Right!"

"Right!"

This was followed by an extended pause while each looked at the other expectantly. Spike then jumped up from his bed and headed for a cupboard, announcing with a knowing look, "I've got something here that will smooth the conversation."

Lynda leapt to the wrong conclusion, perhaps the one she was meant to, and made to leave.

"I *knew* this was a mistake!" She intended it to be her parting shot.

Spike had other ideas. "Hey," he called after her, holding out the box he had taken from the shelf. "I just mean a game of Trivial Pursuit."

Lynda was surprised. "*You* play Trivial Pursuit?"

"Usually on my own. It's easier to peek at the answers."

"What's your best category?"

"I'm hot stuff on Sports."

"I'll blow you out of the water on Art and Literature."

"Try!" Spike invited, throwing the box on to the bed like a challenge to a duel.

The game progressed normally for a few minutes and then Spike asked, "So why talk to me?"

Lynda concentrated on the board. "I like to

know I'm the smartest person in the conversation."

It was Spike's turn. "I bet you say that to all the guys." And after a pause, "Pink!"

"You know what's really strange about the Mystery Writer?" Lynda asked.

"Is that the question?"

"Can you answer it?" Lynda smiled.

"I'll tell you what's strange. If the guy wants to be anonymous, how come he waits till we got a computer? What's wrong with an unsigned letter?"

Lynda was surprised. "I hadn't thought of that. That's a good answer." Trivial Pursuit was not so trivial any more. She dropped the card back into the box. "Throw again."

Spike complied and, as he moved his piece, he continued, "And I'll tell you what else is strange – a competition that no one's ever heard of but us."

Lynda frowned. "Sarah had a theory that it was all done for our benefit."

"Why not? If someone wanted to make sure we had a computer, why not?"

Lynda thought for a moment. "I don't have any good answers to that."

"Must be my turn again, then," Spike said, and threw the dice.

"While you're on a winning streak . . . Kerr said this guy wants to be found."

"Sounds right to me."

"He says there'll be little clues left for us . . ."

"Have you looked?"

Lynda nodded. "At everything that's been sent

to us, every review the Mystery Writer's done. Nothing."

Suddenly Spike was on his feet. "Lynda!" he said. "If that competition was a phoney . . . we were sent more than just reviews."

They looked at each other motionless as the full meaning sank in.

Nothing was said, but simultaneously they made for the door and down the stairs, past a slightly bewildered Mr Thomson who had just prepared a tray with tea and biscuits for Spike and his guest. Spike took a gulp from one of the cups. "Thanks for the tea. See you later, Dad."

As they left the house, Lynda unexpectedly announced that Spike was a genius.

It had been a night of calls and callers. There would be two more – the two most important. First, the newsroom. Spike and Lynda made straight for the item which had been sent in addition to reviews – the photocopy of the advert. It was still displayed on the Operations Board. Lynda grabbed it and spread it out on the hastily cleared surface of her desk. The two of them pored over it. It was Lynda who broke the concentrated silence.

"It's obviously a real page from a newspaper. It's just been messed about with on the photocopier. See how the typeface for the advert's different?"

"Yeah. But it's not telling me anything."

They resumed the examination again until suddenly Lynda spotted something. "Spike! The page number. Look."

Spike read it carefully, but was not impressed. "Twenty-six. I'm shocked," he said, dryly. "I'm stunned."

"Don't you see? This is the photocopy of the right hand half of a double sheet. You can see the centre fold at the side, there, and the edge of the paper there."

"So? All newspapers are made up of double sheets. The right half of this one just happens to be twenty-six."

"But twenty-six is an even number! Spike, the right-hand half of a double sheet is always odd! Look!"

Lynda grabbed a copy of the *Junior Gazette* for proof. She separated the double sheets and spread them out for Spike's inspection.

"One! Three! Five! Seven! . . ."

Spike got the point. "So this was deliberately changed . . . to tell us what?"

Lynda considered this for a moment. "Twenty-six. An address maybe?"

"Great! So we knock on the door of every twenty-six in town!"

"The rest'll be somewhere!" Lynda insisted.

They studied the paper in silence once more. Then something caught both their attention at the same time. Spike moved first, pointing at a cinema advert and reading aloud, "Coming soon to the Capitol Cinema . . ."

They chorused the rest, ". . . *Laurel Avenue*!"

Their quarry had been run to earth. They were off on their final night call.

6.
26 LAUREL AVENUE

Laurel Avenue was in Shortroods, one of the more attractive parts on the outskirts of the town. Fortunately Spike was friendly with someone who lived there and knew which bus would take them there. They didn't speak much on the journey. Lynda was finding the suspense unbearable. At last she would lay the ghost that had haunted her for the past few weeks. She was locked in her private thoughts, remembering the old science fiction programme, wondering just how much they were puppets and who was pulling the strings – and why. There was something quite sinister about it all.

Lynda wondered how Spike felt about it. He certainly hadn't shown all that much interest in the whole business. She stole a look at him, but he seemed quite content – not a care in the world. Actually there was some truth in her verdict. Here they were out at night together and it had been

Lynda's idea. Spike could make good mileage out of that in the newsroom. But more than that, it did please him to be working with Lynda. He reckoned they made a pretty good team. Pretty good? Fantastic!

Their separate trains of thought were brought to a halt with the bus itself as it drew up at their stop. They alighted about a five minute walk from 26 Laurel Avenue. It gave them time to think about what they should say. Suddenly they were there, in front of the house. It stood on its own in a largish garden – altogether an impressive place. It must pay to be a Mystery Writer, Lynda thought.

It was the moment of truth. The two of them looked at each other. Spike was the first to speak. He nodded towards the house.

"Doesn't look like a Mystery Writer's house. You're sure you don't want me to come in with you?"

Lynda shook her head. "This guy likes hiding. Two could be a crowd."

"OK. Good luck. See you back at the café."

Lynda watched Spike wander off. She made her way up the drive, her curiosity taking over from her apprehension, though she had to admit that she was pleased the house was not some great gaunt castle of a thing. It was modern, well lit and welcoming. She checked the name on the door. "Homer" it said. She reached to ring the bell but as she did the door swung open.

"I saw you in the drive. Come in."

Lynda felt quite uneasy as she stepped into the hallway, and all the more so when she was left alone just inside the door.

"Hey! Just a minute," she croaked, after the disappearing figure whom she took to be Mr Homer.

He paused slightly and without turning said, "First on your left."

"What is?" Lynda's croak was getting no better. In any case Mr Homer, or whoever he was, had vanished.

Lynda turned towards the door on her left and approached it nervously. She pushed it slowly open, wondering why on earth she had thought it a good idea to send Spike away.

The room was empty and ordinary enough. There was a bed and the walls were decorated with print-outs of all the reviews. Ordinary enough, that is, if you didn't happen to notice the hi-tech computer system humming on the desk in the corner. She moved slowly over to the computer to discover that it had no keyboard. Instead a strange headset lay before the console. Thoughts of that old TV programme were returning uncomfortably. She reached out to pick up the headset and snatched her hand away at the sudden sound of a series of electric hums and clicks, the kind robots make – and they were getting nearer! Lynda spun round. There was no way out. The thing was definitely coming her way. She waited, her eyes fixed on the door. It was just on the other side. The door was moving and Lynda wasn't doing much breathing. Suddenly the thing was in the room and coming at her.

"You'll understand if I don't get up," Billy Homer said from his electric wheelchair.

Lynda was busy trying to gather her scattered wits and convert her croak back into a voice. "No. Yes." she managed.

"That should about cover it," Billy commented as he propelled the chair towards the computer. "So now you've found me . . ."

He left the question hanging so that Lynda felt obliged to complete it. "What do I want? I want to know something about you – who you are. It's not unusual for an editor to have met the members of the editorial team . . ."

"Well, what would you like to know about me?"

Lynda realized that she wasn't ready for this. "How about your name?"

"Billy Homer. Is that it? Or do you want even more?"

Lynda wasn't doing at all well. "Tell me how you write the reviews without a keyboard connected to the computer."

"Oh, I've got a keyboard all right. It's in that cupboard. Just needs to be plugged in. It's my fingers that are not connected to my brain – and they can't be plugged in."

Quite involuntarily Lynda found herself looking down. His right hand lay upturned in his lap like a dead thing, while his left rested on the joystick which controlled the chair. As though in answer to her unspoken question, Billy moved the joystick and set the chair in motion, round to the computer. The movement was really from the shoulder and not the wrist. Billy explained that he had recently regained that degree of movement, which allowed him to operate the chair.

He sat in front of the computer for a moment and then said, "Well, you wanted to pick it up before." She looked slightly puzzled. "The headset. It won't jump on to my head by itself, you know."

"Sorry. I hadn't realized you wanted it." She lifted the headset and placed it on Billy's head.

"Thanks."

There was a little plastic tube attached to the apparatus, rather like a telephone operator's microphone. He scooped this into his mouth with his tongue and turned towards the computer. Lynda watched, fascinated, as he directed the little arrow around the screen. The slightest movement of his head placed the arrow exactly where he wanted it, and typed by a slight blow or suck on the tube.

Billy pointed the arrow at the top left of the screen, and then pulled it down, revealing a menu from which he selected *Headlines*, and on to the screen came a keyboard on which he could type anything he wanted to.

"You see, I had a keyboard all along," he said. "But that's the simple bit. I can do anything you can do on this computer. And it's all because of a guy called Roy Stringer. He's responsible for this magic machine on my head. It's called Headstart, works by ultra sonics. With this and a Macintosh computer, I could rule the world. Maybe you should put that in your pad and print it!"

In demonstrating the keyboard Billy had typed on the screen, *I AM BILLY HOMER. I AM A TETRAPLEGIC.*

All at once Lynda had a picture for the first time

of the unknown Mystery Writer at his computer talking downline to her on those recent nights in the newsroom.

"And then you'd use the modem and send it straight to the newsroom. That's why you needed us to have a computer!" Lynda said.

"Right. Pencils are so rough on your teeth . . ."

Still with her eyes on the brief statement Billy had put on the screen, Lynda asked, "And you're totally . . .?" She was unwilling to go further.

Billy had no such reservations. "From the neck down I'm history." It was graphic and it was brutal.

"That must be . . . awful." She faltered. Words were inadequate.

"Worse than you can imagine. You don't know what an itchy nose *means*."

Lynda was wrong footed yet again. She looked concerned.

Billy gave her a twisted little smile. "That was a joke. I *do* joke, you know. From the neck up I'm a running, jumping, crazy kid. I just can't get the rest of me to agree."

Lynda was still struggling. Then she thought of something she could say and know it to be true and mean it. "Well, whatever else you are, Billy, you're a fine writer."

This seemed to get under Billy's guard. "I know. And I'm the Mystery Writer. I like that." He was moving back into his secret place again.

"And you're sure that's the way you want to keep it?"

"I like people wondering. I like them not knowing what kind of wreck I am. If Dad hadn't put those stupid clues in, even you would never have known. But now that you have found me, do me a favour – lose me." There was a defensive, almost petulant note in his voice.

"Billy . . ."

But Lynda got no further. "Spare me the lectures on the outside world and making friends. I get enough of that from my parents. And it's kind of unfair on a *really* captive audience."

"Billy, is there nothing I can do?"

"Of course there is. Close the door."

Lynda was grateful even for that small crumb, but when she glanced round she saw that the door wasn't open.

"It *is* closed," she protested.

Billy's face was a mixture of bitterness and self pity. "Behind you," he said flatly.

Lynda did as she was told, but outside she leaned back against the door feeling tired, confused, futile, angry. There were so many conflicting emotions. She was hurt and frustrated by Billy Homer's rejection of her. It was understandable and yet it was he who had forced his way into her life. There was a plea for help there somewhere. She wanted to go back and try again but thought better of it. Then she noticed that the door Mr Homer had disappeared through earlier was ajar. She walked down the hall to find him busy with the washing up. Lynda picked up a dishtowel and started drying.

"The competition was a neat idea," she said.

Mr Homer turned and smiled. "I okayed it with the boss. What's one computer to Roxburgh's?"

"Your son is very brave, Mr Homer."

Douglas Homer stopped washing for a moment and considered what Lynda had said. He nodded in agreement and then added, "I wish he were braver. I wish we could get him down to that newsroom of yours. Get him meeting some people, get him living again . . ." His voice was strained.

After her recent experience Lynda did not feel that was very likely. She changed the subject with a squirt of dishwashing liquid into Mr Homer's washing up bowl.

"You're not using enough of this, the plates are still greasy."

Douglas Homer made a brave effort to deflect the stream of detergent. "I don't like too many suds," he complained.

"But the plates are still greasy!"

"So dry them harder!"

Lynda was defeated. Douglas Homer looked at her, with just a trace of mischief in his expression. "You're just like I was told, you know. Doesn't know what 'no' means unless she is saying it."

Lynda turned sharply, realizing the full meaning of what she had just heard. "Of course! You must have an inside contact on the paper. But who is it?"

"You'd be surprised." He was enjoying this. "I know all about you kids. Colin the money maker. Frazz the nut case. That hoodlum, Spike . . ."

Lynda smiled. "Spike's all right. In fact he's kind of sweet."

Her timing could not have been more perfect. No sooner had she said the words than she knew they were not alone. A third person had joined them. She heard an unmistakable voice quote her own words of earlier that same evening back at her. "I can't tell you how much this means to me!"

At that precise moment Lynda did two things at once. She dropped the plate she was drying and yelped "Spike!" Then, after a pause, "Of course." Much had suddenly been explained.

Perhaps it was the shock of Spike's re-appearance together with the reminder from Douglas Homer about her not understanding "no" as an answer, that activated the stubborn streak in Lynda. Spike reckoned it was rather more than a streak – as did a couple of hundred other folk! Suddenly she knew very clearly she had a farewell visit to pay to Billy before she left.

When she entered his room Billy was busy at his computer and paid absolutely no attention to her.

"A word before I go, Billy. No more Mystery Writer. If you want to stick with the paper, from now on you show your face." If Billy could hear her he certainly gave no hint of it.

"Are you listening?" Lynda pressed on. Her voice was crisp and determined. "You'd better be, because I don't like writers on my team who hide. And I don't like writers who want special deals just for them. Clear?"

Billy continued to behave as though he were unaware of her presence.

Lynda was resolute. "There's a meeting tomorrow night, eight o'clock. Be there! Or just forget the *Junior Gazette* altogether."

Billy raised his eyes momentarily to meet hers but without any acknowledgment in his expression.

Outside his room Lynda paused for the second time that night, her mind filled with doubt. She glanced questioningly along the hallway towards Douglas Homer. He gave her the traditional gesture of approval, the 'thumbs-up'. Outwardly she smiled and shrugged, signalling that she had done her best. Inwardly she prayed she had got it right. Tomorrow night would tell a tale.

7.

LATE!

It was Lynda who generated the tension that night in the newsroom. Naturally enough everybody was interested in the hoped-for unveiling of the Mystery Writer, though most of them doubted that he would show up. To Lynda it went far beyond curiosity or even sympathy for Billy's predicament. The whole thing had taken on a personal dimension. It was as though she was being judged as an individual and that she would pass or fail that test on whether Billy came through the swing doors at the end of the newsroom. It was one of those cases where the longer the jury is out the worse it looks for the defendant – and it had been out too long already.

Sarah watched Lynda. She was like a caged animal, Sarah reckoned, repeating the same routine again and again. She would look unseeingly at the papers on her desk, get up and pace, check the time, sit down – and then do it all again. Sarah knew that to suggest starting the meeting was like sticking her hand in the cage, but someone had to say something.

"Lynda . . ."

As Sarah expected she was immediately one hand short. "*What*?" Lynda snapped irritably.

"Even if he is just late . . . I think we should get started."

"I *know*! I've just got to . . ." Lynda didn't know what she just had to do, but she finished, "Get something." She strode purposefully – but with no purpose – over to where Spike alternated looks at his watch with looks out of the door. In her heart Lynda felt Billy Homer was not going to appear.

"You've known him a long time. Do you think he'll come?" It was as much a plea as a question.

Spike thought for a moment before answering. "I only really knew him before the accident. Now . . . I don't know."

Lynda had hoped for something more optimistic. What she heard confirmed the worst. The fight had gone out of her.

"I can't delay this meeting any longer, Spike!"

"Then start it. If he doesn't come, he doesn't come."

Lynda pulled herself together, accepting the inevitable. She made her way back to the meeting table and took her place at the head of it.

"OK everyone, the first item of business . . ."

"Lynda!" Spike interrupted.

Lynda could usually count on an early interruption from Spike, but this was ridiculous. She turned sharply towards him, and then towards the direction in which he was looking. It was science fiction time again, but this time the now familiar sounds sang in Lynda's ears. They were a fanfare heralding what she most wanted to happen. The doors were swung open and Douglas Homer stepped inside to hold them wide. Into the newsroom rolled the all-humming, all-clicking, Billy Homer, as surly and defiant as Lynda had left him.

Billy's entry was greeted by silence, but every eye in the room turned towards him. Then Spike started to clap, loudly and solemnly. One by one the others rose to face the approaching Billy and one by one the applause spread till the place shook with it. Frazz removed an empty chair and made a place at the table for the Mystery Writer – now no longer a mystery. In the background a very proud and a very moved Douglas Homer watched his son start living again. He let the doors close quietly behind him as he left. It was as if a great cloud had finally lifted.

The first break in that cloud had been when he had watched the impossible at Stoke Mandeville Hospital when Billy had first used Headstart and had found an interface with life. The doctors and nurses who had watched that day had applauded too. They had seen then what Roy Stringer's vision had made possible. This evening in the newsroom of the *Junior Gazette*, Douglas Homer had seen that possibility become a reality. Not since the bleak day of Billy's accident had he felt as he felt now.

Back at the meeting table the applause subsided as Billy guided his chair into his place. He returned in full measure Lynda's steady stare. To others they gave nothing away. Between them everything was said.

Lynda spoke. "Sarah," she said. "Put in the minutes, Billy Homer . . ." She paused and looked back at Billy. He knew what was coming. Just a trace of a smile that touched only his eyes betrayed the Billy Homer behind the mask.

". . . late!" Lynda concluded.

Part Two: HOW TO MAKE A KILLING

8.

THE GIRL FROM WHEREVER

High Point was one of those monuments to modern architecture, a great white tombstone of a building, where people were stacked fifteen storeys high. In the sixties when it was built, they called this brave new idea "the vertical village" but it bore no resemblance to anyone's idea of a sleepy hamlet nestling in the rolling green countryside. High Point reared up out of the town, dwarfing everything in sight – particularly the people. It made a nonsense of what had once been a well-proportioned skyline, as if someone had suddenly changed the scale. And it didn't even save space or money. They had left so much open ground around it – presumably for the inhabitants to use – that a sizable estate of more conventional dwellings could have been provided, and for less money.

Even at the planning stage High Point had attracted criticism but that was nothing compared with the deluge that engulfed it when the tenants moved in. It leaked, through walls, roof, and windows. The lifts, when they worked, were too small to take a stretcher, their doors too narrow for most wheelchairs. It was standing room only even for the deceased – which was the real reason, according to some, that it was called a vertical village. And as for these spacious acres in which the tower was marooned, they were so far below the sky dwellers, and so open to the public, that tenants never used them. Hardly the same thing as a back garden, they reckoned. And as far as the youngsters were concerned, how do you help a hurt child ten storeys away with a lift out of order? How do young children make it to the toilet in time, in the same circumstances? The list was endless.

High Point was an eyesore to most of the older townsfolk, but to Danny McColl it had always been there, just a landmark in a familiar townscape. He eyed it through the viewfinder of his Pentax camera, moving down from the top and zooming in on the main entrance. He read the graffiti. Not bad at this distance, he thought – not the graffiti, the resolution of the lens! It was the first time he had tried the SMC 70–200mm lens, and if the view through the camera was anything to go by it was just the equipment for today's job. Danny was perched on a low wall at the far side of the paved concourse from where he had a clear view of the whole area. He invited Kenny to have a look, to see just how the telephoto range would pull anything or anybody on the concourse into close-up. Kenny was half-convinced. It wasn't so much that he doubted Danny's judgment, just that he wanted to be sure they'd get the pictures clear enough to convince Lynda. Danny shared Kenny's anxiety for clear pictures and a convinced Lynda, though in his case it was to justify the purchase of the new lens, which he had omitted to tell Lynda about! He spoke more in hope than certainty.

"Don't worry about the camera, Kenny. It'll do the job – if there's any job to do." Danny looked at his watch. "Isn't it time she showed up? Do you think she'll come? Is there any sign of her?"

"Yes. Yes. And not yet . . . hold it . . . make that a 'yes' as well. That's her over there by the shops." Kenny's voice betrayed his excitement. Now he'd get his evidence. The girl in question walked into Danny's viewfinder and then accelerated towards him as he rotated the ring on the lens barrel. Danny could see a very good reason for paying attention to this particular subject, though nothing Kenny had said suggested his interest was other than in a good story. The camera clicked and the motor drive whirred briefly. The girl wore a school uniform, not local but familiar, and despite that she was a head turner, by any standards. The shutter flickered and the film shot forward again. Danny tilted the camera and focussed on her blazer badge.

Without moving the camera from his eye, he said, "I can't make out the name of the school but we'll see that on the enlarger." He squeezed the shutter release as he spoke.

Danny zoomed out again to get a better picture of what she was up to. By this time the girl had stopped and seemed to be checking her position in relation to some particular feature of High Point, not that the bland off-white tower had much that could be described as a feature. The finger on the shutter release moved again. Her movements were very methodical as she knelt, apparently unconscious of the rough concrete on her knees. She opened the black briefcase by her side and took out a piece of chalk with which she began to draw slowly and deliberately. The camera clicked and whirred several times.

From this distance and angle it was not possible for Danny to see exactly what she was drawing, but Kenny already knew. The little ceremony was over in a very few minutes and the girl was up and away. Danny took a couple of parting shots, partly for the record, but more so because she was easy on the viewfinder. Kenny on the other hand, without the telephoto benefit of Danny's Pentax, looked thoughtfully at the scene in general, now complete with its chalk image on the concourse.

"Come on," he said. "I'll show you what she drew."

The two made their way across the open square to study the simple line drawing. A surprised Danny saw that it was unmistakably the life-size outline of a human figure sprawled on the paving stones. He photographed it from several angles but said nothing. He knew from Kenny that the girl came to High Point on the twelfth of every month, and performed this ritual drawing. He could see why it had aroused Kenny's curiosity.

"Well?" Kenny asked.

Sarah interviewing Mr Homer

HIGH SCHOOL
NEW ROCHELLE, N.Y.
1897
FALCONS

"Put in the minutes, Billy Homer . . . late!"

"Do you happen to know anything about a girl who draws on pavements over there?"

"You're doing well." "Go shove it!"

Post Office
ESTATE
the Leeds
SPORTING CALENDAR
Stand-ins steer Stones to the top
Borough are so abysmal
Rider in a rage over beating
Lane so close to an upset
Wembley get walloping
Referee robs Lane
EXPOSED! THE SHOPS THA
SELL DEATH!
EXPOSED! PETER'S MARKET
further details of the

"Let's wait till we see the pictures. You'll know more then!"

"Yeah. The school badge should tell us something, and there may be other things we'll notice."

Danny nodded. He was *sure* there would be other things that Kenny would notice! He was also sure that Kenny's impatience to see the photographs meant no tea that night, and Kenny confirmed that suspicion almost the second it was born.

"Let's get to your darkroom," he said, striding off in the direction of the *Gazette* offices without waiting for a reply. Kenny was picking up some of Lynda's less lovable traits, Danny decided.

Once in the darkroom, their roles reversed. There was no doubt who was boss in this territory. Kenny made himself as useful as possible by settling in the corner and giving a reasonable imitation of not being there at all. The normally laid-back dreamy Danny came alive. In total darkness the film was out of the camera and in the tank in no time flat. Kenny screwed up his eyes against the sudden glare as the main light was switched on again. Danny was already pouring in the developer. Within a few minutes the film was out of the wash to be expertly wiped dry between Danny's index and middle fingers.

By the warm glow of the safelight the still damp strip of negatives was placed in the enlarger and the impatient Kenny was soon enough at Danny's shoulder seeing the results of their photographic expedition. "That's terrific!" they both said in chorus, as the image of the school badge formed on the close-up shot. They continued to speak at the same time but revealed a different reason for their admiration.

Kenny said, "She *is* from Macton. That's our first positive lead."

Danny said, "She *is* a beauty. Look at that resolution."

They looked at each other. Both were well satisfied with the day's work. Both had their trump card. Now for Lynda.

9.

OUTLINE FOR A STORY

Billy Homer, as inseparable from his computer as from his wheelchair – buzz-bomb as it was sometimes referred to – had now become a familiar enough sight in the newsroom, and was treated with the same disrespect as all the regulars. For Chrissie Stuart he was still something of a novelty. She had him engaged in conversation as Danny and Kenny made their way past, to confront Lynda. Billy had stopped his work on the computer to answer some questions from the Assistant Editor of the big paper. He still wore his headset as he spoke.

"I was halfway down a hill on my bicycle," he said. "I remember it kind of occurred to me I was going a bit fast." He paused and gave a twisted little smile at the memory. "The next thing that occurred to me was a bus. Then I'm in hospital and they're breaking the news to me about my place in the school football team."

Chrissie, perched on the desk opposite Billy, was finding him difficult to talk to. Her intent serious expression was certainly not normal when she spoke to a member of the *Junior Gazette* team. Billy gave no sign that he noticed. People behaving abnormally was normal for him.

"I was really brave about total paralysis – for the first eight seconds. I was even thinking of a brave little joke while the doctor was giving me my chat. 'Doctor,' I was going to say, 'Not another word about paralysis! I'm up to here with paralysis!' And I'd point at my neck." He paused again and smiled in the same way. "Except, of course, I couldn't."

Chrissie knew that while he was exaggerating, essentially Billy was speaking the truth. She was aware that at the time of discovering about their paralysis, people often react in a surprisingly brave way. Something to do with shock, protective mechanisms and the insulation from reality provided by the hospital surroundings where they suddenly find themselves in a kind of celebrity role. The truth creeps up and takes hold of their minds with greater stealth – and it stays in control. Then the life-long struggle begins.

At just about this point in the conversation the set of damp prints landed on Lynda's desk. She followed the picture story of "The Girl from Wherever" shot by shot, including the finely detailed close-ups. She was encouraged to note these by Danny and, satisfied she had, he returned to tidy up in the darkroom.

Kenny pressed home his views on the story.

"She's from Macton." He pointed to the close-up of the badge.

"Once a month, every month, this girl comes all the way from Macton, goes to the foot of the high flats, draws the outline of a body. Same outline, same flats, every time. No one knows who she is or why she does it. I say we should find out – because I think it's a story."

The ball was firmly in Lynda's court.

The ball was also now finding its way into Chrissie's court.

"Can I ask you a question?" Billy asked.

"Of course," she replied. There was a hint of apprehension in her voice.

"Why are you asking so many questions?"

"I'm building up to the big one. Has Lynda spoken to you about this?"

Billy looked at her for a moment. "Has Lynda spoken to me about you speaking to me? No, I'll have to speak to her." It was more than a tease.

"I want to interview you – for the adult paper. I want to do a feature on you."

Billy's face was suddenly blank and discouraging. "Why?"

"Well, because I think people would find you interesting."

"Why?" There was a flat remorseless quality in his voice.

"Because of the problems you face, the special difficulties . . ."

"What's interesting about that?"

Chrissie was losing ground and she knew it. "Well . . . you're a tetraplegic – completely paralyzed . . ."

It was a pretty stupid thing to say, and she knew that as well. Billy didn't spare her. "Hell no!" He spoke with a pronounced American drawl. "I'm just real laid back!" It was a joke without humour.

Chrissie was rocked by the bitterness in Billy's voice. She hesitated and then asked, with a kind of desperation, "Am I saying something I shouldn't?"

The ball refused to leave her court. Billy continued with his unfunny humour. "Why did the tetraplegic cross the road?"

"Pardon?"

"Come on, it's a joke. Why did the tetraplegic cross the road?"

"I don't know." Chrissie's voice was all resignation.

"He was pushed. Why did he cross back again?"

"Look I . . ." But there was no escape.

"He was pushed. How do you get four tetraplegics in a mini?"

"Billy . . ." Chrissie had never felt so uncomfortable.

"You push them. Getting the point?"

"I don't think I am." Chrissie said weakly.

"I just gave you a day in the life of the completely paralyzed. How do you write *that* up to sound like fun? You want to know how I face up to my 'special difficulties'? Chrissie, what else am I supposed to do?" He left the question hanging and stared at her. Then he delivered his parting blow. As he manoeuvred his chair back round to face the computer he asked, "Walk away?"

It was the only option left to Chrissie. Try as she had she could not get the ball back into Billy's court. It was game set and match to the newest member of the junior news team.

Lynda was happy to keep the ball in her court. It was Kenny who was struggling to get it back. She studied the pictures silently for what seemed an eternity.

"A chalk outline – like they draw round the body in detective films," she mused.

Kenny saw his opening. "That's what got me thinking. Maybe something happened at High Point Flats, an accident . . ."

"A death?" Lynda suggested.

Here came another trump. Kenny slapped down an old edition of the *Gazette* in front of her. "Dead right!" It carried the headline *BOY IN DEATH PLUNGE* alongside a photograph of High Point.

By this time Spike had joined the group and was taking an interest in the discussion. "So a fifteen-year-old kid takes the scenic route to the ground," he drawled. "Is that a reason to draw pictures on the sidewalk?"

"I'm pretty sure it's *her* reason," Kenny answered. "That accident happened two years ago – that's how long she's been doing her drawings."

"But why does she do it? What's the point?" Spike persisted, producing a rather defeated shrug from Kenny.

Meanwhile, with typical thoroughness, Lynda had carefully read the two-year-old article and checked the rest of the paper for further references to the incident. "Interesting," she murmured, half to herself. "The boy didn't live at the flats."

"That's putting it mildly," Spike added, somewhat grimly.

Lynda ignored the interjection. ". . . he just got into the building and then out on the roof, somehow. Fell from there. And did you see this?" She pointed at a reported interview. "There's an old guy who actually saw him fall past the window."

"That's the only fix they have on the time of death," Kenny confirmed. "No one else saw it happen."

Lynda dropped the paper on her desk. "Other than that, it doesn't tell you much, does it? I mean, who was he? Was it an accident? Was it suicide?"

Spike, tasteless as ever, added, "Was he protesting for an outside elevator?"

Lynda, ignoring him as ever, continued, "Did they do a follow-up story?"

"That's the really strange thing," Kenny said. "No they didn't. I went through every edition for the rest of the year – and all I got was about three lines confirming it *was* an accident. I'd call it a big story – but it was just dropped."

"I'm sure there is a perfectly simple explanation, Kenny."

"And is there a perfectly simple explanation for a girl who draws bodies on pavements?"

"What's your point?"

"I think we might be on to something. Why don't you let me follow it up?"

"You haven't sold me on it yet, Kenny. But if you want to make a start I'd suggest the other side of the newsroom . . ."

Lynda responded to Kenny's puzzled frown by pointing to the by-line of the story – *Chrissie Stuart*. "Inside information?" she added by way of an explanation.

Kenny turned to see Chrissie in conversation with Billy. Even from that distance Chrissie did not look at all at ease and appeared to be trying to make a polite exit. She was now standing, having got down from her desktop perch, when Billy had turned back to his computer. As it turned out he hadn't quite finished with her.

"Basically, there's no point," he said, cutting off her retreat. "What good would an interview do? You see, that's the thing about newspapers – they never actually *do* anything. They just write about it. If I'm having a problem, Chrissie, help me – don't just look over my shoulder and write about it."

Chrissie accepted the reproof gracefully. "I'll keep that in mind," she said. "Can I take my feet out of my mouth and say I'm sorry?"

"You'll get over it," Billy replied, and then added ruefully, "I won't."

Chrissie picked up her notebook, looked decidedly awkward – almost as awkward as she felt – and said, "Well . . . see you, Billy."

"Yeah, see you."

As she made her way across the newsroom she

heard Billy call after her. It was yet another joke. "Did you hear the one about the tetraplegic who flew round the world, solo?"

Chrissie shook her head.

"Neither did I." Strangely there was humour in his voice this time – or was it just relief at being rid of her clumsy questions? Chrissie considered this for a moment, turned to go, and walked straight into an eager Kenny in hot pursuit of his story.

"Chrissie, I need a favour. Do you keep your old notebooks?"

Recovering from the near collision and surprised by the question, the best she could manage was, "What?"

"You covered a story two years ago, and I'm wanting some information on it."

Chrissie felt she had spent quite enough time in the junior newsroom for one day, so she kept on escaping as she spoke. "I've got notes back ten years. Come over some time and I'll see if I can help you."

But Kenny was in the "here and now business" and wanted nothing to do with the "some time maybe" approach. He followed her towards the door. "Maybe you remember it. It's about a boy falling off the High Point tower block."

This revelation stopped Chrissie in her tracks. "High Point?"

"You *do* remember." It wasn't a question. It was an accusation.

"Ah, kind of, yeah. Actually Kenny, I don't think I can help you."

"But your notes. You said you've got them back ten years."

"I think I forgot to keep them that time." Chrissie plumbed new depths of feebleness, even for that day!

"And two years later you remember you forgot?"

Chrissie shrugged apologetically and this time made good her escape.

A baffled and highly suspicious Kenny watched her go. He turned to Lynda who had joined him. "Did you see that? Did you *see* that?"

"Maybe she did just forget," Lynda suggested, but it was decidedly lame.

"Or maybe there's something just a little bit funny about this story."

"All the best stories start dull, Kenny. This one's too interesting to be interesting." Lynda warded off what was undoubtedly going to be yet another impassioned plea on behalf of his story. "But yes, you can follow it up!"

Kenny was off in a flash, spilling his thanks to Lynda as he went. She followed him with her eyes. He was certainly determined to see this one through to the end. So be it, Lynda thought – and resumed her other work.

Spike was still thumbing through the photographs when Kenny appeared beside him. "I got the go-ahead, Spike."

Spike nodded and, looking critically at the picture of the chalk outline, commented, "You know, after falling twelve storeys I'd have thought he'd be more . . . spread out."

Kenny joined him in critical appraisal of the outline. "Artistic licence?" he suggested.

"Maybe," Spike conceded. "But it's insane. He

looks like he's lying there pointing, see?"

"You know, you're right."

"Hey, don't get carried away. I'm sure he wasn't really."

"Maybe *he* wasn't . . . but maybe *she* is!" Kenny was already on the move before he had finished the sentence. He called over the noise of the newsroom, "Lynda, I'm just off to High Point. I won't be long."

Lynda made her way over to where Spike stood, still examining the photographs. "He's really got the bug for this one," she said.

Without lifting his eyes but with a deliberate misunderstanding of what she meant, Spike replied, "Well she looks like she's worth getting the bug for!"

Lynda glared at the photo and snatched it from Spike's admiring scrutiny. It wasn't so much the jealousy but the fact that she felt it that upset Lynda's peace of mind.

"I rather doubt that's the reason actually, Spike." It was blast frozen all the way.

"Well, well! Look who's jealous of a girl I've never even met," Spike mocked.

The freezer was still going full blast. "Of course I'm jealous, Spike!" Lynda said, rather to Spike's surprise – and then followed up with, "I wish *I* was a girl you had never even met!"

"She's so crazy about me it's embarrassing!" Spike's rejoinder was a bit late and went unheard. But it pleased him – the idea as well as the repartee. He looked again at the outline of the pointing figure and frowned.

10.
THE SCENE OF THE CRIME?

Kenny found the relatively short trip to High Point unbearably long, so anxious was he to test his new theory. He barely restrained his impulse to actually run. He was convinced the mystery which had become nothing less than an obsession with him, would now be unravelled. Kenny looked down at the chalk outline and carefully moved round until he could line himself up with the pointing finger. He followed with his eyes the direction it indicated, over the paved concourse, across the road, to the shops beyond. That was it . . .? Hardly earth-shaking.

There seemed little doubt that the pointing finger was fixed on one particular shop, a not very upmarket mini-market with the unimaginative name of Peter's Market – the kind of place that sells plastic buckets, tools, general hardware and the like, at what is claimed to be "unbeatable prices." In fact someone had thoughtfully altered the "t" to an "r" so that the sign now read "unbearable prices", which was probably nearer the truth!

As Kenny made his approach, it appeared that Peter, if there was a Peter, was outside the shop tidying up the clutter of "unbearable" special offers.

"This your shop?" Kenny asked in what he hoped would be a casual relaxed tone. It wasn't.

Peter was unimpressed, and his expression could easily be read to say, "Whose shop do you think it is?" Or worse.

"Excuse me asking," Kenny continued in his casual soprano. "Do you happen to know anything about a girl who draws on pavements over there?"

So Kenny may not have got the casual bit absolutely right, but he did not expect it to be quite such a turn-off. One second he was deep in what he had to admit had been a pretty one-sided conversation – Peter hadn't actually spoken – and the next he was chatting up a slammed door!

It was the kind of dead-end that definitely led somewhere, he explained to a not entirely convinced Lynda, who had joined Kenny at High Point, but too late to witness Kenny's interviewing style.

". . . and he turned round, marched into his shop, and slammed the door on me!" Kenny repeated yet again to Lynda as he led her towards the tower block and his other discovery.

"He didn't say anything?" Lynda was a bit mystified too.

"Just gave me a look that could pop your acne."

"Strange – but did you bring me all the way here just to tell me that?"

Kenny firmly shook his head. He had more to tell, but in his own time. "I got the caretaker to let me out on the roof of High Point." He pointed up as he spoke, and the two stood for a moment looking and watching the tower move past clouds. "Amazing how you can get vertigo – on the ground! Want to see the scene of the crime?"

"Crime?" Lynda challenged, but Kenny was already on his way to the lift. She followed.

"Whatever happened to that guy, Lynda, it wasn't an accident," he said with finality.

As the two emerged fifteen storeys above the street and made their way to the front of the building, Lynda asked, "How can you be sure?"

"I'll show you." Kenny led the way up some steps.

"I mean, why not an accident? People have accidents!" Lynda persisted.

"Sure they do. But they don't usually take a running jump at them!"

Kenny gestured to the three-metre-high glass and metal safety barrier that ran round the top of the building. Lynda walked over to see for herself.

"You could pull yourself up on it, drop over," she suggested without much conviction.

"By accident?" Kenny was relentless.

"What are you saying? It was suicide?"

Now the trumps were coming out one after another. "There's a window on the staircase below," Kenny said. If it was suicide he'd have jumped out of that – I mean, why strain your back getting up on one of those things?"

"Yeah, right – who'd want to be dead with a strained back?" It was the best Lynda could come up with – and not bad in the circumstances.

"Come on, Lynda, think about it!" Even Kenny's patience had limits. He held up the fingers of his left hand and counted them off one by one as he listed the extraordinary events surrounding the incident at High Point. "An accident that couldn't have been; newspaper reports that should have been but never were; a girl who draws pictures once a month in the street outside; and a dead guy's finger pointing at a shop where they slam the door if you ask questions. Lynda, I have to keep checking I'm not in a film!" Kenny's voice shifted register from exasperation to a kind of desperate plea. "We've just got to follow this up!"

And he kept up the desperation all the way back to the newsroom, gradually wearing down Lynda's resistance as they went. Lynda led the way through the swing doors. "But how do we follow it up?" She flung the words over her shoulder as Kenny took advantage of the already swinging doors to enter behind her. "You've been trying and no one'll talk to you."

"I just haven't tried the right person yet!"

"And who is the right person?"

"Who else – our Macton pavement artist."

"Kenny, even supposing you could find her, why should she tell you anything?"

Kenny was not to be put off this easily. "I wouldn't go right in asking. I would sort of . . . get chatting to her." It lacked conviction.

"How?"

"I'd think of something," Kenny retreated.

"Kenny, you don't know who she is, where she lives, anything . . ."

This at least Kenny could handle. "True," he said, and then added as though it answered all of Lynda's objections, "But I know where she will be on the twelfth of next month." It was the last of his trump cards and as he played it he slowly pushed one of Danny's photographs of the girl drawing on the paving slabs, rather in the way a cowboy gambler reveals his winning hand.

11.
THE SWITCH

For Kenny it was a long wait until the twelfth, but eventually it came and with it the mystery girl, to renew the chalk outline once more on the paving slabs of High Point concourse. Repetition had made her hand fast and sure and the whole performance had taken on a ritual quality. The drawing done, she picked up her black briefcase and, as always, concluded the ritual with a hard steady stare along the line of the pointing hand to Peter's Market. Then, without a backward glance, she strode off for the station.

Locked in some private world of her own, the girl from Macton was wholly unaware of the lounging figure at the phone box. Danny McColl affected total disinterest as she walked by within touching distance. The minute she passed, Danny sprang to life, grabbed the phone and dialled rapidly as the girl strode on down the street and out of sight. The call was expected and eagerly received on another public phone much nearer to South Park Station. The exchange was brief and the news quickly relayed by Kenny to Spike and Frazz: the Macton pavement artist was on her way.

South Park was a small station, really just a single open platform. It would be a simple matter for Kenny, Frazz and Spike to find their quarry. There was really nowhere for her to go where she would not be immediately spotted. Unfortunately the same applied to the hunters. For Kenny's plan to work it was important that the girl's suspicions were not aroused. Kenny had foreseen this problem and planned accordingly. Spike and Frazz would be the decoys. Their job was to create a diversion and give Kenny the opportunity to substitute, undetected, a duplicate briefcase for the girl's own. Spike and Frazz would take up their positions before the girl's arrival, while Kenny would follow her at a discreet distance. No need for communication beyond the slightest nod. No risk of discovery.

It had sounded good when he had proposed the plan to the other two – foolproof, they had agreed. "But is it *idiot* proof?" Kenny wondered as he watched his fellow conspirators make their way into the station. They didn't have to make a diversion – they *were* a diversion, he decided. He looked at his watch.

"If she is on schedule she'll appear about now," Kenny predicted under his breath, and looked up expectantly. She swung into view, right on time. Kenny felt that mild panic which comes to you standing in the wings when you hear your own cue and there is no going back. Here he was experiencing that kind of "stage vertigo". It disappeared as he fell in behind her. The plan was activated.

By the time Kenny reached the platform the girl was already seated on one of the benches, the target briefcase on the ground by her side. The flaw in Kenny's plan would have been exposed if she had kept it on her lap. Instead that space was occupied by her school hat, a little round affair like an upturned pudding bowl. Further down, draped around a lamppost, the decoys were getting their act together. It wasn't going to be difficult. They eyed her appreciatively – and that part was genuine.

"Hey! You on the bench!"

She heard the unmistakably American voice and turned towards its source to be greeted by rather more vulgar declarations of their admiration – mainly whistles and a surprising compliment for the pudding basin.

"Hey! Love your hat!" It may not have been sincere.

The girl's expression was somewhere between contempt and weariness. With her looks it wasn't hard to imagine that she had heard it all before, though not necessarily in American! Then she turned her head deliberately away. In that moment Kenny deftly switched the cases. He had made his play and the dice were rolling. It was time to wait and see for Kenny and that was something he was not good at.

But it would be worse this time. In that moment when Kenny had swopped briefcases he had also done something else. He had noticed what Danny had seen in his viewfinder, what Spike had seen in the photographs: he had noticed the girl! It was vertigo time again for Kenny and from that brief moment the waiting was going to be a long business.

Everything now had to take its course. Eventually the girl would discover that she had lifted the wrong case. Then she would look for the identity of the owner and phone. Contact! It was beautifully simple – so why was Kenny pacing the newsroom floor driving everybody over the edge?

"This thing is connected, isn't it?" He brandished the phone as he spoke and looked accusingly at the little square socket on the wall.

"It's connected," Lynda muttered flatly, but doubted if the same could be said of Kenny, who appeared to be coming apart at the seams.

"Has anyone tried ringing out? Maybe there's a problem on the line." Kenny persisted.

"There isn't a problem on the line," Lynda assured him and resisted suggesting where a problem could be found.

Kenny's suspicions now centred on the instrument itself. He examined the underside. "Is the ringer turned up?"

"It's turned up."

"So why hasn't she phoned?"

Lynda put her pen down and looked over at the agitated Assistant Editor. "Kenny, stop pacing. She'll phone." Then a thought struck Lynda. "You *did* leave your number in the case, didn't you?" She knew it was an unworthy suspicion as she said it, and Kenny left her in no doubt as to what he thought of it.

He rounded angrily on her. "Of course I left my number in the case! Look, just relax, will you?" With that Kenny was off pacing again.

The last comment had been just a little surprising in the circumstances, and Lynda felt she had better do something. Catching up with Kenny, she placed a reassuring hand on his arm. "Sit down," she said. "Take a deep breath. I've never seen you so worked up."

"I'm fine!" Kenny failed to reassure her.

"Why didn't you wait at home? That's where she's phoning." It seemed logical enough. But Kenny had another plan.

"She phones there, my Mum phones here. I *told* you."

"I know – it still doesn't make sense."

"So talk to my Mum. She wanted me out of the house. She said I was making her nervous."

Lynda's "Can't imagine why!" was thick with irony – and that was a mistake. Peaceful steady Kenny was not acting in character.

"Oh, listen to *her*. Lynda Day – stable human being of the year!"

It was below the belt – round about the knees. Sarah jumped unnecessarily to Lynda's defence. "Come on, Kenny, there's no call for that!"

That was a mistake too.

It was a Kenny high on indignation who now turned on Sarah. "No call for it?" he squealed. "I've been trying to keep the lid on this girl's head ever since I was five years old – and now she says *I'm* worked up!"

Mentioning the five years old bit was a mistake,

and the crisp "Don't exaggerate!" from Lynda should have been warning enough – but this new Kenny was also into kamikaze. He pressed on.

"For twelve years I've been walking behind her picking shrapnel out of people."

"He's exaggerating. He *always* exaggerates about *everything*!"

Sarah had landed herself in the middle of the battleground. "Listen, you two . . ." she protested; but got no further.

"Exaggerating, am I? OK!" Kenny's indignation knew no bounds. "1977, school sports day . . ."

"Oh, here we go!"

"Lynda is six years old . . ."

"I can't believe you are bringing this up again."

But Kenny was remorseless. "Do you know what she does?"

"Apart from winning every event?" It was a bit of casual sniping on the part of Lynda, but there was little else she could do. It wasn't allowed to pass.

"Except one."

Now it was Lynda's turn for indignation and her voice shook with it. "That was badly adjudicated. It was a travesty of justice!"

"Lynda, it was the egg and spoon race!"

Lynda would not be diverted. "And I was a clear two inches ahead of Suzy Bennett! Travis was blind."

"Mr Travis was our teacher," Kenny explained to Sarah and the rest of the news team who had now gathered round. "And he *was* blind – with tears of agony about two seconds later!"

"I can't believe you're stooping this low," Lynda said.

"There he was – with Lynda Day hanging from his leg by her teeth!"

The news team were enthralled and not in the least impressed by Lynda's suggestion that Kenny was being pathetic.

"It's true," Kenny insisted. She went straight up to him and sank her teeth into his leg."

The gladiators were so locked in their combat that only Sarah heard the phone. "Kenny . . ." she began.

"You're just exaggerating again!" Lynda snapped.

"He was all over the playing fields trying to shake her off."

"Rubbish!"

"I saw him in the street the other day – he still walks with a limp!"

While Kenny was enjoying himself at Lynda's expense Sarah had picked up the phone. "Hello, *Junior Gazette*," she said. ". . . Yes, he's here, Mrs Phillips . . . hang on."

Choosing her moment, Sarah intercepted Kenny's attention at the end of his most recent twist of the knife, "Kenny, your Mum!"

Kenny looked puzzled and then remembered the significance of what Sarah was telling him. He grabbed the receiver and scribbled down what he was hearing. He flourished the pad before Lynda and Sarah.

"She's Jenny Eliot and this is her phone number. We've cracked it!"

Sarah was delighted. If nothing else, at least it

might stop Kenny's pacing!

Lynda was still smarting from the injustice of eleven years before. "And did you see the size of the egg they gave me? I mean, do you call that *fair*?"

"Lynda, I got the number."

"It was enormous!" The whole miscarriage of justice was coming back to Lynda, in full. "It was the biggest egg I'd ever seen! I could hardly keep it on the spoon."

"That was no reason to try and force it down Suzy Bennett's throat!"

Sarah tried again. "Shouldn't we just be getting on with the phone call?" Kenny seemed strangely reluctant. This was the guy who had just been wearing out floors waiting for the phone number. It didn't make sense, not to Sarah, not to Kenny. But nothing much had been making sense to Kenny since he had finally got around to noticing the girl from Macton, the girl with the most wonderful name – Jenny Eliot.

Kenny and Lynda paused in their combat and looked at Sarah. Then Kenny sat down at the phone, looked at it, picked it up – and asked, "What should I say?"

"Just what you planned. You've got each other's bags, arrange to meet and swap.

But it wasn't as easy as that, not now that Kenny had noticed Jenny Eliot. If he had admitted the truth at that moment he would have confessed that he had forgotten all about his great story, his investigative journalism, his relentless pursuit of the truth! His voice was plaintive. "Yeah, but . . . what should I say?" he asked again.

Sarah was confused. "What's the problem? She's expecting you to phone her!"

"But it's kind of . . . embarrassing."

Sarah's confusion was rapidly giving way to impatience. "Kenny, just do it. I'm sure you've phoned girls before."

Kenny said nothing.

Lynda saw the opening and was straight in. There was the sweet smell of revenge in the air. "He hasn't, you know," she said. "The only time he ever went out with a girl, I had to ask her."

It was time for Sarah to be stuck on a battlefield again! "Can you believe how childish she is?" Kenny asked her.

Lynda went on. "Ruth Simpson, wasn't it? I had to get down on my knees to that girl!"

"Yeah, and a great job you did too," Kenny muttered, wincing at the memory.

"I persuaded her!"

"Yeah, right! Go out with Kenny Phillips, Ruth – he's dying!" She spent the entire evening crying her eyes out and telling me how brave I was! I was terrified – I kept wondering what she was going to do to me."

Lynda was unrepentant. "Well, you should have asked her yourself! That's your trouble, Kenny – you can't do *anything* yourself. Whatever it is you need me with you!"

"Oh yeah?"

"Absolutely! You can't make a phone call on your own."

"Oh, can't I?"

"Obviously not." Lynda looked meaningfully

at the instrument still lying unused in front of Kenny.

This was too much. His indignation reasserted itself over his embarrassment. "Right!" He grabbed the phone and started to dial.

"This should be good," Lynda goaded.

"It will be," Kenny assured.

"I can't miss this," Lynda mocked.

"You'd better not," Kenny threatened.

"At long last – Kenny Phillips goes solo!"

Kenny would not rise to the bait. As the last digit was dialled he said simply and with a convincing display of confidence – more than he felt – "Yeah! So watch!"

12.
THE LAST STRAW

Jenny Eliot kept better time for her monthly appointments on the concourse at High Point than seemed to be the case with more conventional meetings. Kenny had been sitting for the best part of an hour in the far from elegant surroundings of Czar's Burger Bar. To be fair, Kenny had turned up a bit on the early side – just to be sure he wouldn't be late. He had told himself, and everybody else, that he couldn't afford to miss out on a story as important as this one. Whatever was the truth about his timing, it was certainly a fact that he had chosen Czar's because it was home territory and he would be more comfortable there. "Comfortable" was not a word which normally sprang to mind in connection with the Burger Bar.

Throughout what seemed to Kenny an interminable wait he had kept his eyes on the entrance, waiting for the first glimpse of her passing the window so that he would be ready. Kenny certainly didn't want to be caught off guard. As can often happen to anyone in these circumstances, Kenny's mind wandered and his attention slipped. Actually he was wondering just how he would greet this goddess who had agreed to meet him. He tried not to remember how he had set the whole thing up and that she was coming really to meet her briefcase. On the other hand, and to his credit, he tried not to forget *why* the meeting had been set up.

The sudden bump of a briefcase alongside the one already on the tea-stained plastic tabletop in front of Kenny brought him abruptly out of his reverie. Suddenly she was there before him. Kenny made a creditable effort at standing up, allowing for the fact that it was not really possible to straighten up without first sliding out of the bench seat he was trapped in. And he couldn't really do this because Jenny Eliot was blocking the way. Kenny settled for a kind of crouch which gave the appearance of taking cover behind the briefcases. From this position he emitted a rather weak "Hi!" It was a great start!

Jenny eyed him coolly for a moment or two and then returned the "Hi!" An awkward silence followed, doubly so for the crouching Kenny, and then "So . . . ah . . . I'm Kenny Phillips," he offered.

"I know," she replied. "I phoned you."

"Oh, right, yeah." Kenny's laugh was distinctly uneasy. Things were getting worse by the second!

"And you're Jenny Eliot."

Jenny knew that too and she confirmed that she still was.

Kenny was raising discomfort to an art form. Jenny regarded him wryly and did nothing to help.

"Look, I'm sorry to drag you all the way here. I could've gone to Macton just as easily."

Jenny wasn't letting up. "Now he tells me."

Kenny was immediately on the defensive and flustered. "But you said . . . on the phone you said . . ."

"It's OK, I'm joking." The relief was short-lived. Jenny was off on another tack. "Lucky thing you left your phone number in your case," she said. "Almost like you expected to lose it." She was checking through her recovered case as she spoke, but brought her gaze up to meet his for the last bit.

"Oh, no, I . . ."

She stemmed his stuttering flow with a gesture and a smile. "Relax! I thought it was very clever of you. And flattering. No one's ever wanted to meet me so badly before."

All through the conversation Kenny had been digging holes for himself. Now he threw himself in, head first, and pulled the dirt in after him. "I didn't want to meet you!" he announced and then rushed on, "I mean, I didn't want *not* to meet you, I just . . ." He tailed off hopelessly. Ace reporter? Great lover? Perhaps Lynda was right.

And Jenny wasn't finished with him yet. "Either way," she said. "You've got as far as buying me a coffee."

That really threw the already bothered and

bewildered Kenny. "I haven't bought you a coffee."

Jenny's "I noticed," told him that perhaps he should have.

"Oh, sorry. Please sit down." Kenny sat too and at last escaped from his crouch. He turned in his seat and summoned the waitress in as masterful a tone as his present condition would allow. "Ah . . . excuse me . . . ah . . . could we . . . ah . . ." It seemed to work.

The waitress came over. "Hi, Kenny," she smiled.

This was easier. "Oh hi, Maria." And then to Jenny, "This is Maria." Thank goodness it wasn't Anastasia, Kenny thought. It was the first thing that had gone right for him. Nobody would believe "Anastasia" in Czar's Burger Bar, but that was the other waitress's name.

Jenny acknowledged Maria and Kenny completed the formalities by introducing Jenny as "Ah . . ."

She provided her own name, "Jenny – still!"

Kenny pushed on through his own personal minefield offering the titbit of information that Maria was a waitress. It evoked a rather dry "Really?" from Jenny. Kenny then turned his attention to ordering, securing a coke for himself and, with some prompting from Jenny, her cup of coffee.

Home territory could have its drawbacks, especially for a guy set on showing just what a man of the world he truly is. Out of the blue Maria the waitress enquired, "Straw with the coke?"

It was like a bombshell to Kenny – and when

you're already digging holes in a minefield, that can be bad!

"No!" It was more a denial than an answer.

"You usually have a straw," Maria insisted.

"No straw, thanks." Definitely a denial.

"He usually has a straw," Maria assured Jenny, who nodded with understanding.

"I don't want a straw." The denial had a strangled quality now and was delivered through gritted teeth.

Maria conceded. *No straw* she wrote on her pad.

Kenny's "Thank you!" sounded like escaping steam.

Suddenly Maria remembered. "We've got the bendy ones," she said, hopefully.

"No! *Please*!"

Jenny had great difficulty in maintaining something like a straight face through this interlude, but by the time their coffee and coke-with-no-straw arrived she had regained her composure. By this time too Kenny had remembered that he had a job to do. He made a clumsy start.

"You know, I keep thinking I've seen you before."

"The station?" Jenny suggested.

"No, not there," Kenny continued the charade. His face brightened with sudden recognition. "Have you ever been near High Point Flats?"

It was terrible stuff – not only the world's oldest chat-up line, but some of the world's worst acting too.

Jenny went quite still and looked intently at Kenny. He could sense that she was on guard.

"You could have seen me there, yes," she said, giving nothing away except perhaps a warning to keep off.

If it was a warning then it went unheeded. Kenny stumbled on, like someone moving downhill on loose scree, unable to stop. "Drawing, maybe?"

Her eyes narrowed. "I'm a pavement artist." Her voice was suddenly icy.

He had come this far . . . In for a penny, in for a pound. "You don't have pavements in Macton?" he asked.

"What is this – coffee or interrogation?"

"Just trying to make conversation."

"Would it help if you pointed a light in my face?"

It was time to retreat. "Hey, I'm sorry, I didn't mean to —"

"Well, you did . . ." she flared and Kenny ducked. He was quite deflated, and sat staring into his half-empty glass wondering what to do next, how to remedy the situation. It would all have been so easy if she hadn't turned out to be . . . to be Jenny Eliot; if it had just been another story.

She looked at him and relented. "Hey! I'm sorry. You picked a bad subject." Then she changed subject to dispel the gloom. "It was deliberate, wasn't it? Switching the cases." There was mischief in her voice.

Kenny's guilt wouldn't allow him to admit anything. "Oh no, I don't know how it happened," he lied and hated himself for doing it.

She smiled. She knew it had been deliberate and all the denials in the world could not alter that.

"It's OK – really. Quite nice in fact."

Kenny liked hearing that. But what he was doing was not at all nice. What a mess. For the moment he tried not to think about it. The accounting would come later.

"You could just have spoken to me at the station, you know," Jenny continued.

"Or I could have followed you home!"

"Yeah! Maybe my mother would've let me keep you. She goes for the cute type."

They were enjoying each other's company now but "cute" – that was too much for Kenny's self-image.

"Cute?" he enquired.

"The teddybear look," Jenny explained. This was getting out of hand!

"You think I look like a teddybear?"

"What's wrong with that?"

Kenny thought about that for a moment or two. "I always thought I was more kind of mean and moody."

"Mean, moody – and a bit like a teddybear." It was as much as Jenny would concede. But she smiled as she said it, and that made all the difference. They both laughed.

They bantered on some more but, as with all good things, the end came in sight much too soon. Kenny's plea was plaintive, though he phrased it as a question. "You've really got to go?"

"I'm late already. And after all the trouble you went to getting me here – sorry." It was sincere.

Kenny was right in there, with all the dash and decisive drive of a dead jellyfish. "Look, ah . . . I was wondering . . ."

Jenny Eliot genuinely didn't have time for this. Probably she didn't have the patience either. "There's a film coming to Macton I wouldn't mind seeing," she prompted.

"What film?" Kenny asked, unhelpfully and quite irrelevantly.

"I've no idea!"

The penny, one of the slowest on record, dropped. "Oh, right! Well, look, why don't we, ah . . . go and see a film . . . you know . . .?"

"Together?" Jenny prompted.

"If you think that is a good idea," Kenny said, decisively.

"Well, we could go and see a film separately but together saves on popcorn. How about Tuesday night. Tuesday good for you?"

"It's getting that way," Kenny purred.

"Come by my house about seven – you know my address. I'll see you then."

"Yeah, see you Tuesday," Kenny agreed.

Jenny Eliot turned to leave Czar's – and then hesitated and smiled to herself. Kenny was bathing in the warm glow of total contentment that had enfolded him since the moment he realized he had a date with Jenny Eliot. He leaned back, his hands clasped behind his head.

Suddenly, Jenny was beside him again, just long enough to drop a bendy straw in his glass and wink. Then she was off. Kenny, who had long forgotten he was an ace reporter on a mission which he had at one time thought to be earth-shaking, tilted himself forward in his chair, took the straw between his lips and blew a stream of bubbles into his coke.

But moments of such contentment were not common on the *Junior Gazette* and the earth was hurried beneath Kenny's feet again by a familiar voice at his elbow.

"Terrific, Kenny," Frazz said from the table behind. "You really grilled her!"

13.
A CHANGE OF HEART

Chrissie Stuart was surprised by Billy Homer's message. After her recent encounter with him she had decided that articles on Billy were to be a distinctly no-go area, and though she understood his feelings the whole business had not made her feel at all good. She couldn't make up her mind which troubled her most – whether it was the insensitivity that she had displayed in blundering in, or the loss of a feature important not only to the *Gazette*, but to those people who suffer the same disability as Billy, but have neither adjusted to it as well nor have the benefits of the amazing Headstart. If the article did no more than inform people about this, it would be sufficient. But to have been able to share with her readers the story of Billy's recent success in coming to terms with the world at large . . . This was heady stuff.

Right from Billy's first appearance Chrissie had been deeply impressed. Here was a young lad, keen on sport, as active as any, whose world had been suddenly shattered by the dismal prospect of a lifetime spent in a wheelchair, dependent on others for everything, a lifetime of total paralysis. Yet now he was a fully-fledged member of the news team with no quarter asked or given. The paper had been set up to do something about the kids who for one reason or another were not realizing their talent. This kind of problem had never been envisaged by Mr Sullivan at Norbridge High when he had inspired the idea of the newspaper that would be a voice for youth, but Billy must rate as one of its most spectacular successes. His was a story which had to be told.

There was no doubt about Billy's personal courage. That was evident in his immediate and total dismissal of the very idea that anyone could be interested in the slightest way in what he obviously regarded as his own unremarkable story. There was also no doubt about the part the *Junior Gazette* had played. Mr Homer had made it abundantly clear that without the challenge and opportunity the paper had offered, Billy would have had increasing difficulty finding enough purpose in living. Even more important had been Lynda's seemingly harsh demand that in the news team there would be no special cases or conditions – even for Billy Homer. It had been a bad moment, make or break time, but Billy had made it. It was the difference between being part of the world and withdrawing from it – until what had begun as privacy soon became isolation, and courage was eventually overwhelmed by despair.

And there had been another ingredient, the one

which had made the others technically possible – Headstart. Chrissie had never been what could be described as a computer enthusiast! It was in the nature of her work that she would become familiar with word processing and in her own nature to extend that necessity to a much wider understanding of computing. But to see Billy at work on his computer had been a whole new experience. For the first time the power of a microcomputer was really serving someone in a truly important way. It put the person in "personal computer".

She had made up her mind to do an in-depth feature on Billy while she had watched him working away at his desk in the junior newsroom. She had been hugely impressed with the special programme Billy used in the computer. He was able to exploit a whole range of word processing, number crunching, business management, music composing and arranging, even design and graphics programmes, as well as the next person – who didn't happen to be in a wheelchair. The more she had learned about Headstart, the more she had seen of Billy, the more Chrissie had become convinced about the importance of her feature. It had been a severe blow when Billy had dismissed the idea so quickly and so emphatically. Now it appeared there might just be a reprieve. Chrissie got up from her desk. She hesitated a moment, looking at the notebook lying on her desk and then scooped it up. She was feeling lucky.

Chrissie found Billy in the newsroom – or rather he found her. She was still trying to locate him amid the usual bustle when she heard from the other side of the room, "Did you hear the one about the tetraplegic juggler?"

It was Billy and he was still at his jokes – but the earlier bitterness had gone. "I think I am about to," Chrissie replied as she made her way towards him.

"He was lousy. Kept dropping the tetraplegics!"

Chrissie winced. "Did you ask me over just to tell me that?"

Billy smiled. "I've been doing some thinking – well, there's not a lot else I can do – and if you're still on for that interview, I am too."

"Why the change of heart?"

"Well, it's better than sitting here twiddling my thumbs," he said, and then added, "I imagine!"

Whatever the reason, Chrissie was delighted and impatient to get on with it. "I'm glad to hear it. How about if we start right away – if that's OK with you?"

"I'll cancel my skydiving. Now, how did the tetraplegic get back to his desk?"

Chrissie was not to be caught out this time. She moved round to the rear of Billy's chair. "He was pushed," she said, doing just that.

14.
LIFT OFF!

There was of course a very good reason for Billy Homer's change of heart, though it was doubtful if Chrissie would have greatly appreciated it. Their conversation did not go unobserved. Lynda's eyes had never left the pair for one moment. As Chrissie started to push Billy, Lynda's face relaxed in relief. "She's gone for it. Get moving!"

It was the order Julie Craig and her graphics team were waiting for. Lynda walked with them towards the door, giving final instructions as she went. "Remember, she keeps her old notebooks in the bottom drawer of her desk." She was referring to Chrissie. "If anyone asks you what you're doing, just say she sent you to get something."

The small group moved quickly and unobtrusively, past the engrossed Billy and Chrissie, out of the newsroom and over to the main building. They were lucky. No one saw them and they were soon settled at Chrissie's desk behind the security of a closed door. Lynda's suggested cover story should see them through should anyone come in – provided it wasn't Chrissie. Then it would be the suicide pills!

The communication line for the undercover graphics team was Frazz. He kept on the move watching for signals warning of an imminent return to base by Chrissie and keeping Lynda posted about progress.

Frazz returned to the newsroom, passing close enough to Chrissie and Billy to check what stage the interview had reached before reporting Julie & Co's progress with the old notebooks. Chrissie was asking about the maps Billy was working on in his computer and he was deep into an explanation of the visual database of the town that he had been constructing. Chrissie was mesmerized and would stay that way for some time. Billy was doing a great job as a decoy.

As Frazz approached her, Lynda asked, "How much longer?" She was referring to the "research" into Chrissie's notebooks.

"Julie says we'll have everything copied in another half-hour. She's got the whole graphics team working on it. By the way, we know the dead boy's name."

"Yeah?" Lynda was immediately interested.

"Yeah." Frazz was still Frazz. This could take time.

After a brief pause Lynda said, "And are you going to tell me what it is, Frazz?"

Frazz thought about this and it looked for a moment as if he might just have forgotten what he was expected to tell Lynda. Then he recovered. "Oh! Right! Michael Eliot."

"Eliot?" It was almost a challenge.

"As in Jenny Eliot's brother," Frazz confirmed. "Might explain why she turned pavement artist."

As Lynda reflected on the likely significance of this information Sarah appeared at her elbow.

"Lynda, have you got a moment?" She was carrying one of Danny's photographs and a photocopy of Chrissie Stuart's original piece in the *Gazette*. "I've been doing some thinking. The only evidence for the time of death is the old man who saw the boy – Michael Eliot – fall, right?"

Lynda nodded and Sarah pressed on. "Suppose the old man just made it all up for a bit of excitement, or imagined it, or something."

"What put that into your head?"

Sarah pointed at the photo. "The position of the body. The only windows he could have fallen past would be on the stairwell."

Lynda shrugged. "Maybe the old man was on the stairs when he saw him."

"That's what he says in Chrissie's notes." She held out the photocopy. "He was on his way back up to his flat, he'd been out."

It seemed straightforward enough to Lynda.

"Lynda," Sarah said. "What's an old man doing going back up to the twelfth story by the *stairs*?"

At last the fog cleared. "Instead of the lift! Of course! Check it out – you could be on to something."

Sarah cleared up that particular little mystery

very quickly. She telephoned the gentleman concerned, who was fortunately still living at High Point. She thanked him for his help and as she replaced the receiver, her expression told Lynda that once more they were getting nowhere. "He did remember why he took the stairs all right," Sarah said. "But I don't think it's going to make the headlines. He got out of the lift on the tenth floor because – hold the front page – it smelled!"

"It smelled?"

"Like a cleaning lady's bucket, really strong. There was a cleaning lady around at the time, it adds up."

"To nothing," Lynda concluded, with a sigh. "I always said the best stories start dull. This one was far too interesting!"

"What now?" Sarah enquired.

Lynda thought for a moment. "Put it all together on the Operations Board and we'll see what we've got. We may have missed something." Lynda did not sound at all convinced. It was more a case of "When you can't think of anything better to do, do what you can think of!" Or put another way, "Don't give up!"

Later the news team gathered round the meeting table opposite the display on the Ops Board which Sarah and Julie had prepared. In the centre of the board was a large scale drawing of High Point. Danny's photographs were all there in sequence along the top and now included one of Peter's Market. Lines had been drawn to connect various features to slips of paper which contained what information they had gleaned. Optimistically, the marker pen had been left primed and ready for that further inspired connection which would crack the problem and give them their story. The faces of the news team suggested otherwise.

After a lengthy silence, Sarah said, "Chrissie had a ton of information in her notebooks. It just doesn't make sense that the story was dropped, no follow-ups."

"Did she have anything on the shop – Peter's Market, or whatever it's called?" Lynda responded, but there had been nothing.

"So we still don't know why Jenny Eliot draws her brother's body on the cement." It was Spike who summed up their lack of progress.

He had overstated their level of information and Sarah pointed this out. "We don't even know for certain that it's her brother. Could be a cousin or something."

Lynda picked up from where Sarah had left off. "*And* we don't know how Michael Eliot came to fall. *Or* what the connection is with Peter's Market. *Or* why the *Gazette* didn't keep with the story. We don't even know why Chrissie lied about losing her notes." Lynda thought for a moment and then continued. "To date, out first attempt at investigative journalism has established one fact – on 12th September, two years ago, there was a smelly lift."

15.
FLYING HIGH

Kenny had returned to the newsroom from his meeting with Jenny in Czar's while the news team were still in discussion. He had not felt inclined to join in. Instead he nursed the straw Jenny had given to him and chatted to Billy, who was still busy at his desk.

"The thing is," he confided in Billy, "it's not fun now. At the start it was a mystery to solve, it was exciting. Now it's just like poking my nose into somebody's personal business. And I'm lying to her." There was a sigh in his voice which turned to self-condemnation. "I feel like a total rat."

Billy was conciliatory, which was a bit out of character. "Everyone feels like that sometimes."

"Yeah?" Kenny, always ready to see the good side of himself, began to think that perhaps he wasn't really a rat after all.

"Sure," Billy continued. Then, leaving just enough time to let that idea grow, he added, "The number of times I've felt that you're a total rat . . ."

While Kenny smiled ruefully at Billy's swift return to character, his straw was removed from his hands. Kenny whipped round to hear Frazz's voice.

"The one she gave you? Talk about clutching at straws . . ."

Kenny was not amused and snatched his bendy straw back. "I just happen to like straws," he said huffily.

"Sucker! Anyway, the news team is stuck and you're supposed to be helping – says Lynda." The "says Lynda" added a great deal of authority to Frazz's invitation.

Kenny accepted – if somewhat gloomily. "Headline – *Rat Returns To Sinking Ship*," he muttered and trudged off over towards the rest.

Frazz extended his invitation to include Billy, but that was rejected. Frazz pressed him. "Hey, it's a big story. We're trying to crack the mystery."

Billy remained unimpressed. "I know. Trouble is, I don't see why it's any of our business."

Lynda was still encouraging her team when Kenny arrived to take his place. ". . . so the only thing we can do now is to get out there, get our feet on the pavements, get some interviews at High Point . . ." She broke off to greet the prodigal Kenny. "Where were you?"

"I was talking to Billy," Kenny replied.

"Kenny, this is your story!" Lynda reminded him.

But Kenny was unrepentant. "Actually, it's

Jenny Eliot's story . . ." he started irritably but was interrupted by Frazz who had developed a habit of coming up behind him at the wrong moment. He had been learning bad habits from Spike.

"Well, if you'd spent some time questioning her, instead of just gazing into her eyes . . ." Frazz said, more or less directly into Kenny's ear.

Kenny swung round. "Maybe I should have taken my tape recorder and press badge!" His sarcasm was lost on Frazz.

"You couldn't have done much worse!" Frazz said, contriving to make it sound as though he considered it to be a reasonable suggestion.

"I've had enough of this!" Not irritable now, just plain angry. Kenny turned to leave as he spoke, but Lynda had different ideas.

"Kenny, you've got a story to do," she snapped.

"So what?"

"So why have you suddenly gone like this?" Lynda demanded.

Kenny looked at her wearily. "Because yesterday I felt like a real hot shot reporter . . . and today . . . I don't know."

"Kenny, we're just trying to bring something out into the open," said Sarah. "It might even do some good."

"What good? Sarah, we'd do as much good with a feature about *why* that lift smelled like . . . a . . ." Kenny's voice tailed off and his eyes opened wide. ". . . like a cleaning lady's bucket!" He stopped, mouth and eyes both gaping.

Lynda watched, intrigued. "Kenny?"

But Kenny was in a world of his own. "That's it!" he exclaimed.

"What?" Lynda was still broadcasting, but it was a case of "Come in, Kenny. Is there anyone there?"

"Not an accident, not suicide . . ."

"You know how he died?"

There was just a flicker of reception but it was obviously a very weak signal. He looked vaguely towards Lynda from inside his private world. "Poor Jenny!" he said, but it was not to Lynda.

"You know how he fell?" She was still transmitting.

Kenny glanced briefly at Frazz and then turned and marched straight for the door. Lynda was after him in a flash, slamming the door shut again as he pulled it open. "Kenny! You know?"

He turned his eyes towards her. "I'm going home," he said firmly.

Sarah had caught up with the two of them. "Why is this business getting to you?" she asked, her voice earnest and concerned.

"Because this business is none of our business," Kenny snapped. He opened the door to leave.

Lynda promptly slammed it again. "Kenny, you *know* – how did he fall?" It was a final demand.

He considered her for a moment. Then he resigned himself to answering this tiresome query. "He didn't fall, Lynda," Kenny said. "He *flew*."

The door closed behind him on a silent and bewildered news team.

16.

A NEW ASSISTANT EDITOR

Another day, another dollar, Spike reflected, from a semi-recumbent position at his desk, feet higher than his head. Whatever that means! The newsroom, at least, was normal – which meant that special mixture of chaos and useful purposeful activity – in far from equal proportions. And it was Saturday. Everybody behaved differently on Saturdays. Frazz had his Saturday bewildered look on and was protesting to anyone who would listen. "I can't believe it! I've been doing the astrology for six months and nobody tells me Purple isn't a sign of the Zodiac."

As far as Spike could tell he was the only listener. Julie was answering the phone. It was for Colin. A Saturday phone call, this should be interesting, Spike decided, but his attention was distracted by Lynda's voice from directly behind. "Any word from Kenny?"

"Two," Spike replied. "The second one was 'off'!"

Lynda about-turned rasping, "Terrific!" She headed off in the direction of Sarah's desk. Spike concentrated on Colin.

"Henry!" Colin acknowledged his caller warmly. "I haven't seen you since we fixed up that little deal with the fourteen faulty prams."

Here we go, thought Spike, a Saturday special – and he was right. Colin's expression was rapidly losing its warmth. "Well, it must have been a very heavy baby!" he said defensively.

Julie was on the move again. Spike caught sight of her as she passed behind Colin. She was pursuing Danny, demanding to know how many "f's" there were in "photograph". Her spelling had not improved. Nor had Colin's phone call. "Henry! What use would I be to you dead?" His tone was distinctly aggrieved now.

Lynda's was pleading. She had found Sarah and seemed to be chasing her round the desk. "Please, Sarah! Kenny's been gone for two days. I need an Assistant Editor!"

It was all from the heart but Sarah was not relenting. "See that pile of work," she said, pointing. "Somewhere under it is my desk!"

"I wouldn't ask if it wasn't an emergency!" The pleading was giving way to blackmail. It was no more successful.

"I've got three stories to do for the next edition, two cinema reviews, and so much homework I won't get to bed between school days!"

Lynda accepted unaccustomed defeat with her usual good grace. "You don't know what you're doing to me, Jackson!" She spat the words at Sarah and turned on her heel.

Spike's attention returned to Colin. Things were getting worse. "I was going to deliver the brakes. What did she leave it on a hill for anyway?"

Spike was conjuring up a picture of what Colin's last protest may have been about. Prams without brakes. It was pretty horrendous even by Colin's standards. He didn't get far. Lynda was beside him again.

"Spike!"

"Lynda!"

"Kenny's gone and I need a new Assistant Editor."

This was a new twist in the Kenny/Jenny saga. It wasn't all bad. It certainly must be Saturday. "Hey, yeah?" Spike prompted, enthusiastically.

"Could you stand in till I find one?"

Better and better. "I'm going to be Assistant Editor?" Spike savoured the idea.

"*Acting* Assistant Editor, temporary," she added – or subtracted, depending on how you looked at it.

"Is that better?" Spike was definitely into addition.

"It is for me. Come on."

Spike followed Lynda but took time out to let the whole newsroom know his good fortune as seen from his very particular point of view. "Now she makes me Temporary Acting Assistant Editor. Is that a come-on or what?"

Lynda definitely plumped for the "what".

"Spike," she hissed. "You weren't exactly my first choice!"

But Spike was seeing the best in everything, particularly if it got to Lynda. "Well, that's encouraging," he said. "Out of everyone you don't like, I'm your favourite."

For once Lynda did not accept that as a challenge, perhaps because they had drawn level with Tiddler who had been watching the duel with that mature tolerance that only the very young possess.

"Having another little disagreement are we, children?"

"No!" "Yes!" Spike and Lynda, in that order, disagreed simultaneously.

"That's a good answer," Tiddler conceded, and moved out of range.

The sparring continued at Lynda's desk. "Right, Spike! You use the desk next to mine. The top drawer of the filing cabinet is my territory, the second top's yours."

"Gotcha, boss."

Lynda ignored Spike's response, and the fact that he kept smiling at her in that whimsical little way he reserved for her annoyance! "And try and remember – although we've got separate in-trays, we always use the same out-tray."

"Does that mean we're engaged?"

This time Lynda decided on confrontation. "Spike, do you know what's going to happen if you keep cracking jokes?"

"What?"

"You'll say something funny!" Spike was wounded, and staggered around clutching his pierced heart. "She's cruel, she's so cruel!"

"I get worse," Lynda said, knowing she had won that round and seeing the opportunity to get back to work. She produced a great sheaf of papers and photographs from one of the drawers.

"These are Kenny's notes on the High Point story. Get them in order, trim them down, and give them to the first one on the writing team who's free – except Tom, he's an idiot."

Spike glanced at the bundle and looked questioningly at Lynda. "But it's only half a story. All mystery, no answers."

This was hardly news to Lynda. "So if you've got no answers you make the questions bigger." Lynda flipped through the bundle and pulled out a picture of High Point Tower and proceeded to demonstrate how to keep the article running on questions rather than answers.

"Two years ago Michael Eliot falls from the very top of High Point Tower Block. It's called an accident – but how could anyone accidentally fall over a three-metre-high glass and steel barrier?" Lynda pointed to the barrier. "Use a close-up of the barrier," she added.

"Then speculate a bit. If it was suicide, why didn't he take the easier ride out of the open window below?" Again Lynda pointed and suggested a close-up. "Did he climb another staircase just to make it harder on himself?"

Catching Lynda's drift, Spike selected one of Danny's photographs of Jenny Eliot, Pavement Artist. "What about his sister?"

Lynda looked at the picture for a moment. "The best bit. Every month since her brother's death, Jenny Eliot comes to High Point and draws the outline of his body on the spot where he fell, one arm pointing at a row of shops. Why does she do it? What does she know?"

Spike was impressed but couldn't resist being Spike. "Do I include the bit about the ex-Assistant Editor figuring out what happened and not telling us – and then walking out on the paper because he's gone nuts for Jenny Eliot and doesn't want to turn her into a newspaper story on their first date?"

Spike had the right idea but definitely the wrong material. Lynda didn't actually say all that. One word was enough, delivered in that special way she reserved for bringing him to heel. "Spike . . ."

"Only asking." All meekness and innocence.

A new voice joined the conversation. "Did you hear about Kenny?" It was Danny, and his timing wasn't all that it could have been.

"I don't want to hear that name again unless it's attached to an insult."

Lynda meant it, but Danny was not deterred. "I saw him going into the station after school – twenty past four."

"So?"

"Well, the next train is at four-thirty."

"So?" Spike's "So" was even more impatient than Lynda's.

"So first stop Macton – and Jenny Eliot."

It could mean nothing or everything. They looked at one another. Time would tell, Lynda thought. Yes, time. "Do you know when he got back?"

"Seven o'clock train," Danny said. He had gone back to the station to take some photographs after tea and had seen Kenny returning. They hadn't spoken. Kenny's expression had suggested that it wouldn't have been the best idea and Danny was already in a precarious perch trying to get a good angle for his shot. Why was it that the sun, if it was there at all, was always behind the subject?

"So he was back on the seven o'clock that night?" Lynda murmured, thoughtfully.

Danny read her mind. "And if you subtract the time for both journeys, he couldn't have been in Macton for more than an hour and a half."

"Not long enough for a date," Lynda chimed in. "So, if he was seeing Jenny Eliot, he must have been working on the story. But if he's working on the story why isn't he working here?"

Danny shrugged. The Kenny/Jenny story had plenty of questions and plenty of hints. It was answers that were in scarce supply.

"Thanks anyway, Danny," Lynda said and straightened up from the filing cabinet at which she had been working. She had a handful of files which she dumped on Spike's desk. "You've only been in the job for a few minutes. How do you do it? All wrongly filed!" She pointed at the bundle. "Spike, most people can spell the *alphabet*!"

Spike looked stricken. "Don't tell me! It's got two l's."

17.

WHAT A DAY!

When Kenny had stormed out of the newsroom, he was quite clear about what he had to do – at least in part. Having suddenly understood the reason for Michael Eliot's death, he knew the story had to be written. That was a responsibility he had to face. How else could he be true to himself? For the same reason he could no longer sustain the deceit. He would now have to confront Jenny with the truth about himself, that he was a reporter in pursuit of a story. His trick to meet Jenny was to get closer to that story. He could hardly expect her to be overjoyed at this revelation – but the softer options were worthless.

Most of the time in school the following day was spent thinking about what had to be done, fearful of it, anxious to do it. The lesson periods were punctuated by an uncharacteristic frequency of reprimands for inattention.

Mr Sullivan was suspicious that a commitment to the *Junior Gazette* was playing some part in the sudden waywardness of one of his best pupils. Moments like these always caused Bill Sullivan a brief bout of self-doubt. Mrs Samson took the less charitable view that he was just going the way of all the others – particularly the motley collection who worked on that "newspaper thing". Lesser teachers didn't really notice anything to be accounted for, didn't really notice pupils at all – well, not as individuals. They saw them as a collective threat to be contained.

The long day did eventually end and Kenny made a beeline for the South Park Station. He was ten minutes early and had time to remember the last time he had been there. It seemed incredible that only a matter of hours had elapsed since then. How could so much have changed?

The train was bang on time and Kenny was soon enough approaching Jenny's house. It wasn't quite what he had expected. The street itself was obviously upmarket, to say the least. One of those places where you don't really see the houses, just driveways leading round bends. He found Jenny's simply enough. Her directions were good. Even in these surroundings, it seemed almost out of place. Kenny found himself letting out a long low whistle of appreciation. Jenny Eliot was one rich little lady.

None of this made it any easier. What do you say to a butler? He pressed the bell and stepped back. It seemed the respectful thing to do. The door opened more quickly than he had expected. Kenny had imagined that the butler would approach at a more dignified pace. But it was no butler. Just a smiling Jenny Eliot, and just as incredible as he had remembered.

"You're ten minutes early," she said. "Ten minutes and five days."

In normal circumstances Kenny would have joined in the banter but he had a job to do. "I know what happened to your brother, Jenny. All I need to know is why nobody will talk about it – and why you draw on pavements."

Jenny's expression didn't so much change as vanish. She was thunderstruck.

Kenny hurried on. "Can we go for a walk or something? I don't want to talk in front of your parents."

Jenny blinked, and her expression hardened into anger. "What makes you think I'm going to tell you anything?"

Kenny took from his inside pocket a folded newspaper. Jenny took the paper and looked at it. She unfolded it to reveal the masthead – *Junior Gazette*." For a few moments she looked from the paper to Kenny and back. Her confusion was obvious, as was the slow dawning of what it all meant. Then she slammed the door in his face.

Kenny was defeated. As he started to leave, the door was suddenly flung open again. "Don't move! I'm getting my coat!" Jenny flared at him.

The two of them set off down the street, Jenny striding out ahead, Kenny struggling to keep up. "We're going a bit fast, aren't we?" he suggested.

"I'll say we are," Jenny snapped back. "I can remember when you were just some sweet guy who took the wrong schoolbag."

"You didn't even believe that at the time."

"I also wouldn't have believed you were only after me for my dead brother."

This was getting them nowhere. Kenny started, "Jenny . . ." He got no further, not with Jenny under full sail!

"Listen, if that's what you're into, I can set you up with a girl with *two* bereavements. Sort of double date!"

That hurt. Kenny countered. "Can we talk now or have you got anything else smart you want to say?" For him that was pretty crisp and it had the desired effect – at least to the extent that it stemmed the flow.

Jenny spun on her heel and glared at him. "You talk. I'll listen," she commanded. "You tell me how you know what happened to Michael."

Kenny was knocked off his stride. "You mean I shouldn't know?"

"Are you kidding? Look, my Dad's a rich man, he's got all the right friends. He had that story killed in every newspaper that so much as glanced at it. So how come the boy reporter knows the whole thing?"

Jenny's tone was far from friendly and the last bit stung. "The boy reporter worked it out!" Kenny flung the words over his shoulder as he walked away from her, knowing she was bound to follow.

"How?"

Kenny didn't break stride. She would have to keep up to hear what she had to hear. "An old man used the High Point lift just after your brother. He said it stank like a cleaning lady's bucket." Kenny stopped and turned to face Jenny. "Which got me to thinking. Suppose your brother was sniffing solvents in the lift – it'd explain the smell. Suppose he was going up to the top of the building for a bit of peace and passing out. Suppose he was so high by the time he got there . . ." The directness of Kenny's language reawakened in Jenny the old pain and she turned away. "I've heard of it happening," Kenny continued, his voice softer. "Kids so high on that stuff they think they can fly."

Jenny remained silent, her face still turned away. He was intruding on her private grief. He had no business there.

Kenny went on. "My guess is he climbed on one of the barriers and just took off. The ground must have come as a bit of a surprise."

Jenny stood for a long moment, her expression set. Then she said, "Go home." Her voice was flat, lifeless. Kenny didn't understand. "Go home, Kenny," she repeated. "Now!" She walked away.

Kenny stood his ground, angry. "I don't understand you, Eliot," he shouted.

"I know," she flung back at him.

Kenny started after her, still shouting, frustration welling up. "You spend two years drawing your brother's body on the pavement right where he fell – you spend two years *trying* to be noticed . . . And when somebody *does* notice, what do you do?"

This was too much for Jenny. She swung round, her eyes flashing. "You're right I wanted to be noticed! The trouble is, boy reporter, you noticed the wrong thing!" She fired the words at him, and was gone.

This time Kenny did not feel inclined to follow. He stood for a moment, his eyes closed in private despair at his own lack of tact, at his inability to help this girl who had come to mean so much to him. He resigned himself to failure as a reporter and as a person. He headed for the Macton West Station and the lonely ride back to town.

After his return from Macton that Thursday Kenny's mood was so gloomy that his parents and his sister spent most of the evening asking him, in rotation, what the matter was. An irritable "Nothing!" or "I'm fine!" was the best they could expect in reply. In the end Kenny went off to bed early – a popular move as far as the rest of his family were concerned.

Throughout much of that restless night Jenny's words rang in his ears, as he drifted in and out of a disturbed sleep. ". . . you noticed the wrong thing . . . you noticed the wrong thing . . ." Steady and insistent like a drum beat. It was a challenge, a demand even, which he could not put aside. Whatever else he may have been unsure about, at least Kenny now knew that there could be no turning back. He had a lot of thinking to do and by the early hours of the morning he had decided on his next step. It was only then that a more tranquil sleep came. He would not return to the newsroom until the Saturday morning. Saturday suited his plan better. Then there would be a whole day stretching ahead of him uninterrupted by school – a day in which to meet Jenny's challenge.

18.
SEEING THE POINT

Lynda was just thanking Danny for his help over the timing of Kenny's Thursday night jaunt to Macton, when the swing doors of the newsroom opened just enough to allow the ex-Assistant Editor to make a discreet entrance. Kenny stopped just inside the door where the shelving partly concealed him from the view in general and Lynda in particular. He looked carefully round the room.

Kenny's entrance had not gone entirely unnoticed. Frazz and Tiddler were engaged in checking out the horoscope feature, Frazz reading the star signs, Tiddler confirming they had been completed. It went something like this.

"Virgo?"

"Check."

"Scorpio?"

"Check."

At that precise moment Frazz caught sight of

the intruder. "Kenny!"

"No, no I don't think I've got that," said Tiddler.

At about that same moment Kenny found where Billy was and made straight for him. His greeting was acknowledged by a dry, "Oh, look! Here comes history."

Kenny ignored it. "I need to talk to you," he said.

Billy chose to misunderstand "What's the problem?" he enquired. "Did you try everyone who *could* walk away first?"

Kenny still ignored it. "Remember that business I was telling you about – High Point Tower Block and Jenny Eliot?"

Billy reckoned he'd had a fat chance of forgetting since it was all that anyone talked about. He had even given Chrissie an interview so that her office could be raided, but he kept all this to himself and continued in his previous style. "I remember you fancied one of them."

Kenny would not rise to the bait. "I told you I felt like a rat because I was lying to Jenny. And I got the feeling you thought I was a rat too."

"Whatever gave you that idea?" Billy replied, all smiles. "Roll up your tail and sit down." While Kenny found himself something to sit on Lynda was well into her review of Spike's first few minutes as Assistant Editor, Acting, Temporary, Unpaid – unaware of Kenny's presence.

". . . and why's Jeff on the school story instead of Sally?" she asked.

"Sally had to go home," Spike offered, reasonably.

"Had to *what*?" It was like a whiplash. "Spike, we've got rules about people ducking work!"

"Yeah, I know – only four grandparent funerals per person. She was sick. I had to let her go."

"Did you use a thermometer?"

Yeah, it's Saturday all right, Spike thought. Out loud he said, "Hey, you didn't tell me I got to do physicals!"

"I've got to have *proof*, Spike."

"So I'm told. Is it true that you made a guy bring his tonsils home from hospital?"

"Lynda!" Sarah's voice interrupted them. She was pointing in the direction of Billy's desk.

"Does this mean I'm fired now?" Spike asked.

"What's *he* doing here? And what are they talking about? Did you get close enough?" Lynda demanded.

"Sorry." Sarah hadn't.

Lynda pressed on. "Spike, have we got anyone who can lip-read?"

"Well, no . . ." Spike began.

"Then why not?" As Lynda spoke she sidled closer to Billy and Kenny.

Spike could not answer that. The question was unfair. He appealed to Sarah who assured him that was just what Lynda was like. Part of her essential charm. Perhaps Frazz was right about him always going for the bossy ones, Spike thought.

As Lynda edged closer she felt something warm and decidedly alive at her feet. She looked down to see Colin cowering under a desk. In answer to her not unreasonable enquiry into the precise purpose of his behaviour, Colin said simply but urgently, "Lynda, if a guy comes looking for me with a pram wheel could you tell him I've moved to Canada?"

Lynda shook her head and concentrated on Billy and Kenny. She was out of earshot, their voices being too low to carry over the general hubbub.

"The wrong thing . . .?" Billy pondered.

"That's what she said – that's what I noticed."

"So how can I help you?"

Kenny's reasoning was simplicity itself. "You think I'm a rat for what I did – so does she. Maybe you can tell me what I'm doing wrong."

"Well, speaking on behalf of the stared-at, I can tell you this. When you're in pain what you don't want is somebody making a newspaper story out of it." As Billy said it, he remembered his decoy interview with Chrissie. Was his pain that much less, now that he had rejoined the world? Well, maybe!

"But she *did* want to be noticed," Kenny insisted.

"But *what* did she want noticed? Maybe not herself, maybe not even her brother . . ." Billy's voice slowed down, thoughtful now. "The drawing was pointing, wasn't it?"

"Yeah. At a shop."

"Where he bought the solvents?"

"Yeah, could be!" The thought was growing in Kenny's mind.

Billy went on. "It's illegal to sell that stuff to the under-age, you know."

Kenny was up with Billy now. "And the

shopkeeper sold it to Jenny's brother!"

"And made a profit out of killing him. So the dead finger points at the murderer," Billy added.

It was coming clear to Kenny now. "That's it! That's what she's trying to say!"

"It's a protest – against the guy that killed her brother!"

"And nobody's doing anything about it!" Kenny was on his feet. "Billy, you're a genius."

Billy smiled. "What little of me works is solid gold," he assured Kenny.

So far so good, Kenny thought, but he needed proof. In the words of his science teacher, Mr Sless, "A hypothesis without experimental confirmation is useless". It was time to get the confirmation. "I'll need to get out to the shop, and talk to the guy . . ."

"Well, before you do . . . got a photograph of Jenny?"

Kenny reacted as though it was an accusation rather than a request.

"Well, Danny took some pictures . . ." he mumbled, obviously embarrassed.

"I'll settle for the one you've got on you," Billy replied, perceptively. He studied the photograph Kenny took out of his pocket, and then said, "Now that is seriously female. She'd have any guy stockpiling the zit cream."

"Yeah, she's nice, isn't she?"

Billy agreed and then said, "Christine Adams."

He had lost Kenny just for the moment.

"Girl in my class at school when I still had a few working parts – so good to look at she could wear your eyes out."

Kenny was intrigued. "This a Reader's True Romance? I love those photo-stories but my sister keeps forgetting to buy them."

Billy warmed to his subject. "She used to keep looking at me – you know? Like maybe she . . ."

Now that the spotlight had transferred to Billy, Kenny relaxed. "Fancied you?" he suggested.

"But I couldn't be sure. I mean, didn't dare try anything in case I was wrong. So I had a little idea. I was going to leave a note in her desk and all it would say would be 'Dear Christine, This note is from the guy you fancy most.' I reckoned that the first thing she'd do after reading it would be to *look* at the guy she fancied most. And if it was me, I'd be past the tape, the crowd would be cheering, and I wouldn't be a *bit* embarrassed!"

"Did it work out?"

"I never got round to trying," Billy confided.

"Why, what happened?"

"You're looking at it. I took a bike ride to intensive care." There was a flatness in Billy's voice. As Kenny looked at Billy he saw again the helpless crumpled figure in the wheelchair, the one you lost sight of when you were chatting away cheerfully or were too wrapped up in your own problems. Kenny had no idea what to do or say. He just stood there awkwardly.

He stumbled into, "Yeah, well, I . . ."

Billy smiled and released Kenny from his misery and embarrassment. "Listen, you'd better get to that shop. It'll be closing soon." Kenny glanced at his watch. It was much nearer to lunchtime than he had reckoned. "Yeah, right. Look, thanks Billy."

"No problem – good luck with the lady. And, ah . . ." Billy grinned and switched into a mock American drawl, "Don't go downhill on no bikes!" Then he added much more briskly, "Look, get moving, will you?"

"Yeah, sure! See you, Billy!"

Kenny's determined and swift exit did not escape the eagle-eyed Editor. She was after him in a flash.

"Kenny!"

As she passed Spike, barely installed at the Assistant Editor's desk and already packing to leave, she stopped. It was almost impossible in the junior newsroom to complete anything you started without a series of detours – particularly if you happened to be Lynda Day. "What are you doing?" she demanded.

"Well, I thought if Kenny was back . . ." Spike didn't get far along that line.

"Think for yourself only when I *tell* you!" she advised.

Sarah watched the exchange with a smile. She stepped over to Spike and laid a comforting hand on his arm. "Never mind," she said. "Maybe *next* time she'll fire you."

This digression had cost Lynda her contact with the escaping and increasingly elusive Kenny. She hurried after him out through the main doors and straight into a large gentleman brandishing a pram wheel.

"We'd like to speak to Colin Mathews," he said threateningly. Lynda had given up her chase and stopped. She looked beyond the man to see who "we" might be. "We" turned out to be a substantial queue of substantial women, all apparently with an interest in Colin's health – but a distinctly negative one. Significantly they carried their babies and wheeled an unimpressive array of what even at a distance were defective prams!

19.

PETER'S MARKET

Inside Peter's Market, with its still "unbearable" prices, things were pretty much as Kenny had expected. It was a rather seedy, run-down place with shelves not quite as full as they might have been, with goods too often of unknown origin. Whether, this time, the man behind the counter was Peter, Kenny had no way of being sure but he was relieved to discover he was not the same man as he had met on his previous visit. Not that this individual was any more welcoming than his predecessor had been.

Clearly Kenny must have given every appearance of being a shoplifter since Peter, or whoever it was, frequently stopped reading his newspaper to cast a suspicious eye in his direction. For his part Kenny was making about as good a job of being a casually browsing customer as the greasy unshaven specimen behind the counter was of being a public servant. Yet another piercing glance prompted Kenny to pick up something as though he might be thinking of buying it, as opposed to stealing it. When his eyes and mind came into focus, Kenny discovered that he was holding a very cheap and definitely female shampoo. Some shoplifter, he thought.

Swinging round in what he reckoned was a suitably casual manner, Kenny approached the counter. "Ah . . . excuse me . . ." he tried. It produced a pretty bleak response from the paper-reading proprietor, if proprietor he was. But who else would dare read a newspaper while on duty? The watery stare unnerved Kenny just a little and he hurried on. "You don't know me," (that could hardly have been a surprise to the man with the watery stare.) "But a friend of mine used to come here. He used to ah . . . buy glue." Then after a pause. "Solvent based," he prompted.

The effect of Kenny's nervous embarrassment was only to confirm in the mind of the shopkeeper his true purpose. He nodded with sly understanding. "No problem."

Moving only his right arm he reached below the counter and produced a small screw-top can of glue. He set it down before Kenny with the kind of "nod and a wink" which meant it was the real McCoy, vintage stuff! "Two pound fifty," he said and placed it in a plain brown bag.

As Kenny left the shop with his purchase he removed it from the bag and examined it with a real sense of disbelief. Was it this easy? Billy's hypothesis had withstood the test. The pointing finger had at last been heeded. Now he could tell Jenny.

He was already late for lunch and the *Junior Gazette* could wait a bit longer. He decided to go directly home. He phoned Jenny from there.

"Hello, Jenny?" he started, hearing the familiar voice on the line. "Sorry, Mrs Eliot, you sound really like your daughter. Is she there, this is Kenny Phillips . . . Is that what she said about me? I suppose I can understand that . . ." he continued, putting a brave face on things, despite a bad review. "And that . . . And that . . . Yeah, and that too." All the reviews were bad. "Listen, Mrs Eliot, could you give her a message? Could you just tell her I've noticed the *right* thing now." Kenny hesitated, looked at the glue container, and then went on. "I don't know what I'm going to do about it yet, just that I've noticed it . . . No, that's all." The last bit was in reply to an "Is there anything else?" from the other end.

Kenny almost had second thoughts but thought better of it. He signed off, put the phone down and sat back in his chair.

He didn't feel satisfied. There was more he'd like to have said. He decided to have third thoughts and started to dial again.

In Jenny's house at the same time, the hand that had just replaced the receiver lifted it again. The voice had been indistinguishable from Jenny's voice and the hand too bore a striking resemblance to Jenny's hand – hardly surprisingly since it was in fact Jenny herself who had taken the call! She was also rethinking and had decided to phone back. Their timing was bad. Both got engaged signals and both replaced the receivers firmly, with disappointment mingled with irritation.

Next stop lunch and then we'll see what Lynda Day has to say for herself, Kenny decided. It was a hungrier and more sociable Kenny who joined the rest of his family for that midday meal. For them that was a welcome change from the restless pacing soul who had replaced their normally placid Kenny. Fed and watered, he left the house in a cheerfully purposeful frame of mind for the afternoon stint at the newsroom.

20.

THE BIG ONE

By the time Kenny arrived at the paper that afternoon, Spike and Lynda had been having an extended go at each other. It had started with one of Lynda's little notes. Spike found it on his desk. It said "File Two, distribute rest. L." No "please", no "thank you", none of the conventional common courtesies which a guy like Spike expected, was accustomed to. What the heck, he always threw piles of papers in the bucket anyway, on the basis that if they were important he'd get another one.

Having dropped the offending note in the bin Spike found himself staring at a second note which had been underneath the first. It said "NOW!" in capitals. Perhaps on second thoughts . . . Spike wearily gathered up the stack of papers and expressed his feelings for his Editor as a Game Show host, loud and clear but to no one in particular.

"Hiya, folks. This is your old friend Spike Thomson. Welcome to the Miss Dreadful Human Being Contest – and our first contestant is Lynda 'Heart-of-Teflon' Day."

Spike had to interrupt his oration because Lynda was at his side. "Tell Dennis we're cutting the giraffes and tell Colin I can add up and not to try that again. And move a little faster, Spike, we could end up going monthly!"

For Spike this was a kind of last straw. He was at the risk of becoming hen-pecked, all because of his recent acting temporary so-called promotion. He fixed Lynda with a cold and menacing stare of the kind he had used in his less savoury days to some considerable effect. "You know, I used to have a kind of tough reputation around this town." This was true. Spike had been and still could be quite a formidable individual. "I was once attacked by five other guys," he went on. "And nobody would believe *they* started it!" This was only a slight exaggeration – there were a few people who didn't know the Spike of old who would have believed it!

True or false, the boast cut little ice with Lynda. "You've been telling that story since there were only *two* other guys," she said.

Spike eyed her darkly as she moved off and resumed his Game Show hosting. "Lynda's favourite colour is obedience. That's true, folks. And her favourite pastime is biting off dentists' drills."

Sarah had joined the Game Show audience. "She can be hard, can't she?"

"Hard? Listen, they had to use an industrial

laser to pierce her ears." Spike was really warming to his subject.

"Her ears aren't pierced," Sarah protested.

"I didn't say it *worked*!"

Some of the effect of the punchline was lost in the delivery as Spike's eye caught something unusual over by Colin's desk – or rather where Colin and his desk had been, when last seen! "What's that?" Spike asked, pointing at an enormous, but scarcely identifiable, tangled heap of metal and plastic.

"It's a pile of prams. Some stuff Colin picked up, I think," Sarah informed him, not strictly accurately.

Spike was concerned, almost frantic. "My God!" he gasped. "What did he do with the babies?"

In front of the prams sat Colin, though it has to be said that under them would have been preferred by the dissatisfied customers who had brought back the defective merchandise. He was at his most dejected – a figure of despair, his head plunged in his hands. Any returned goods were bad news for the entrepreneurial Colin. On this scale it was disaster.

Kenny noticed neither Colin nor his prams as he strode through the newsroom. He had eyes only for Lynda Day. Her first hint of his presence was the sudden arrival of a squat little can of glue on her desk, followed by a curt introduction. "High Point jump juice. One whiff of that and you fly straight at the ground!"

Lynda studied the can, revolving it slowly in her hand. She lifted her gaze to meet Kenny's. Her expression was shrewd. "Let me guess," she said. "He was high enough to think he didn't need anything under him?"

"He was right for the first ten floors," Kenny replied, his grim humour adding a certain force to the comment.

"It's a good story," Lynda concluded thoughtfully as she studied the little container again. Then, with mild accusation in her eyes, she transferred her scrutiny once more to Kenny. "Good enough to walk out over?" she asked.

Kenny side-stepped the question. "Its a *great* story. It's a *wonderful* story. But forget it, because I've got something better." Kenny spoke with complete conviction. He lifted the can and held it out towards Lynda. "Getting away with murder."

Lynda leaned back in her chair. It was certainly a big story, perhaps too big.

Lynda's attention was momentarily distracted by an unaccustomed amount of activity at Spike's temporary acting desk. A glance was sufficient to tell her that he was eagerly packing up to make way for what he took to be the returned Kenny. Lynda looked pointedly at Spike, who promptly started unpacking. She said, "What have I told you about thinking for yourself?"

Spike smiled wryly. "Well I don't *believe* it gives you cancer," he declared.

She returned her attention to Kenny, who had not missed the point. It wasn't exactly welcome home for the prodigal yet. "OK. Talk!" Lynda said.

And talk they did, long and hard. Exploring all

the possibilities, all the consequences. There was so much to gain, so much to lose. Between them they painstakingly hacked out a plan of action. It took time but in the end the decision to go with the story was taken. It would be by far their most ambitious yet, the riskiest, the most dangerous, the most worthwhile. This was the big one. They had to get it right.

21.
PREPARATIONS

"OK everybody, listening time!" Kenny shouted the words from a vantage point on a large packing case. The typical newsroom rabble came to order more quickly than usual at Kenny's command. They knew something serious was afoot. The pressure from Lynda for them all to be there and punctual warned them it would be no ordinary day. And the rumours had been flying. But so far nothing for certain was known. It was Kenny's story and Lynda intended that he should lead.

Kenny went on to give a broad outline of the strategy and then launched into a detailed series of instructions, mostly to do with reorganizing the newsroom and allocating particular duties. He wound up, declaring, "As of now, every story for the next edition is cancelled. We've got something big to do, maybe the biggest thing we'll *ever* do. And your cooperation will be more than appreciated. It will be compulsory!"

This rousing call to arms was immediately followed by a mighty crash. Kenny spun round to see that the dissatisfied customers had finally got their preference. "And could somebody get Colin out from under those prams?" he added. Kenny stared for a moment in wonderment at the buried Colin and then turned back to his audience. "Let's get this show on the road," he said, jumping down from his makeshift platform and joining Lynda, who had been leaning against the packing case throughout his little speech. "Well, Boss, we're on our way," he said, as a great wave of activity swept through the newsroom.

Desks and tables were being cleared of typewriters, trays, papers, and then dragged together to form a single expanse of work surface in the centre of the room. Two boys brought in a wide roll of tan-coloured paper. As they passed Lynda she said, "Not big enough." They executed a neat about-turn and disappeared out again.

Frazz was acting as a kind of stage manager in charge of the new layout. His voice could be heard above the others, shouting instructions in general, and in particular asking, "Could you clear four more desks, please? We need another four." He followed this with a request for three chairs, which was greeted by three rousing cheers! He also got his chairs.

Not all the team were in the furniture moving business. Others were undergoing their basic preparation for what lay ahead. Spike had installed himself shopkeeper-style behind a desk as a counter. He was trying to persuade Sarah that it was all necessary. "Sarah, everybody has to do this!"

"But Spike . . ." Her plea fell on deaf ears.

"Everybody!" Spike insisted. "Now let's try again – and remember, you're mean, you're tough, you're hard! Now ask me!"

Sarah braced herself and approached Spike at his counter. "Could I buy some solvent-based products, please?" she asked, all polite and demure.

Spike groaned. He prowled around Sarah, trying to find inspiration. "You're hard, you're 'street', you're mean to old people, you get up from the table without asking permission, you eat jam doughnuts without wiping your mouth afterwards! Sarah, you are *bad*! Now give it to me!" Spike had dug deep in his search to find the bad Sarah. He had put his heart in to it. Professor Higgins never had it this bad with Eliza.

"Could I buy some solvents?" Sarah said, and with a definite edge in her voice. Spike saw hope – and saw it vanish as she added "Please!"

This time he wailed in real despair. It was going to be a long day.

The paper carriers pirouetted again and disappeared when their second roll of wide tan paper also failed the Lynda test. She was on her way over to the prams when she rejected it. No one else having responded to Kenny's rescue appeal on behalf of Colin, Lynda thought that as Editor she should take on the responsibility – and besides, she needed a full team for this project. To be fair, everybody was pretty busy. It was something to see.

Julie and Tiddler were deep in discussion over a drugs abuse leaflet. "We'll just need to put some spots round their mouths and get them to look dopey," Julie suggested, pointing at an illustration of a young lad who had been using glue as non-sticky stuff.

Tiddler smiled. "Believe me, we've got 'looking dopey' licked!" She looked round to find the perfect model. "Frazz!" she called.

When Lynda got to Colin she discovered the true nature of the problem. It wasn't so much that he was actually *trapped* under the prams, more that having got there, he preferred to stay there! His life was in ruins and things looked better through a slowly-turning pram wheel. The problem for Lynda was trying not to laugh. Adopting as sincere a manner as possible she said, "After a mess-up like this, Colin, you need to get involved in something that'll improve your image."

"My image is fine," Colin replied, petulantly.

"Are you kidding?" Lynda was aghast. "Listen, you can't afford mistakes with babies. Ask any politician who's dropped one!"

Kenny was on the phone. Mrs Eliot's voice was definitely identical to Jenny's. "Yes, Mrs Eliot. Listen, could you just make sure Jenny gets the next edition of the *Junior Gazette*? Thank you very much." As an afterthought he added, "You know, Mrs Eliot, you do sound very like your daughter."

Lynda's idea of a change of image for Colin was not proving at all attractive. "No way, Lynda! Some of these shops advertise with us!" His protest was heartfelt.

So was Lynda's exasperation. "Do you ever think of anything except money?"

"Sure!" Colin insisted confidently.

"What?" Lynda demanded.

Colin went into deep thought, long enough for Spike, only a pace or two away, to have reached the closing stages in the training of Sarah – without noticeable improvement.

He was all but on his knees during the final phase, pleading, willing, exhorting. "Sarah . . . from now on you're a different person. From now on you never use words like 'please' and 'thank you'. OK!"

Sarah nodded penitently. "Sorry, Spike," she said.

Spike screamed quietly. What he said was not too clear, which was probably just as well!

By now Lynda reckoned that Colin might have an answer. "Well?"

"I'm trying to think. It was a long time ago," he said, earnestly and indignantly. As he said it a germ of an idea was developing in his head – about money, of course. Perhaps Lynda was making sense – not that she would realize it. Time to join the world again and get on with taking it over. To Lynda's surprise, he started to burrow out.

Lynda had spent too much time with him anyway and moved on. She caught a glimpse of Spike's face, glowing with pride as he all but conducted, note by note, Sarah's new-found talent. It shattered before her eyes as Spike sunk on to the floor, a defeated person. "No!" he shrieked, as he went down. And then, crumpled and weak, "Don't curtsy," he begged, but it was a plea of despair.

But not all was uphill. A roll of wide tan paper big enough to please even Lynda had been found and was now spread over the large work surface in the middle of the newsroom. Two of the graphics team were crawling over its surface putting the finishing touches to a huge town plan. In the centre was a rectangle proudly emblazoned with the words "JUNIOR GAZETTE OFFICE".

22.
LET BATTLE COMMENCE

The newsroom had taken on the appearance of one of those Fighter Command Operations Rooms from which the Battle of Britain gets won over and over again in old movies on TV. Round the table were a number of the news team under the direction of Lynda.

The remainder were out in the field, more commando than fighter pilot. Only their faces were not blacked – they were spotted! One of these greater spotted news kids was already in Henderson's General Stores, over in the south east of the town, sniffing, eyes watery and spots around the mouth. Closer inspection, if anyone had felt inclined, would have revealed that it was Frazz. He held out a small squat can of glue not unlike the one Kenny had got. "I'll take this," he muttered, brandishing a fiver in his other hand.

The shopkeeper looked at Frazz carefully, and at the glue with the same attention. Frazz pushed the fiver forward and the shopkeeper looked again at Frazz and took the money. He rang up his little transaction on the till and returned with the change to Frazz, who took it and then walked smartly to the door. He put two fingers in his mouth and let out a piercing whistle. The shopkeeper, to say the least, was taken aback.

"Hey!" he shouted, suspecting an imminent mugging. "What is this?"

Into the shop ran Danny, camera at the ready. The shopkeeper was about to be well and truly mugged – but not quite in the way he might have expected.

"Can I ask you why you think it is all right to sell dangerous solvents to an obvious glue-sniffer?" Danny got an excellent series of close-ups as the motor drive zipped its way through confusion, panic, anger, and a number of unidentifiable contortions, particularly when Frazz removed one of his spots which was halfway to detaching itself.

"What is this?" the bemused shopkeeper repeated.

Frazz smiled. "*Junior Gazette*," he said, and left abruptly. He had a lot of shopping to do that day!

Danny followed and signalled a thumbs-up to Spike, who was leaning against one of the phone boxes in the shopping precinct with a clipboard in his hands. It was his first hit, and duly noted.

The second came close on its heels. Sarah appeared behind him brandishing a bottle of cleaning fluid. "Got it in the supermarket," she yelled. Spike dispatched Danny to the supermarket.

"You're doing well," he assured her.

"Go shove it!"

"That's my girl!" Spike said admiringly. He turned and reported in by phone.

When the call was received at "control" a counter marked "*HIT*" was raked into position on the town plan over Henderson's Stores by Kenny. Lynda walked round to meet him. "Lisa just phoned in. No hits in Dover Road and they are just moving into Weston Street."

Kenny adjusted some pieces to show their new position. "They should meet Spike's team about halfway down," he said.

Lynda watched the board for a while and then announced that Roger's bunch were moving kind of slow and would never make it to Benton Ford. Kenny suggested that she scared them into action on their next phone call. He was insistent that all shops must be covered.

A young lad, one of the *Gazette*'s latest recruits, appeared behind Kenny carrying an armful of tubs and cans and aerosols. "I got them in Charlotte Street. Where do I put them?"

"Number Eight," Kenny told him. He turned and headed off towards Colin's prams, which were no longer a heap but now laid in a neat line and each one numbered. He deposited his purchases in Number Eight. The use of the prams, for filing the "contraband" in geographical order, was a good idea – but it was not Colin's. The idea that had come to him in his moment of inspiration under the prams was more in his style. That it was put into action was due to panic on Colin's part at the plan Kenny and the others had for him! No sooner had he emerged from his temporary prison, than Kenny was greeting him with, "Great, Colin. Get made up and hit the street." It didn't sound at all good – and it got worse. Kenny had called Julie over to take charge of the make-up. He was led off by the two of them.

"Made up as what . . .?" he demanded to know.

"A glue sniffer, of course." Kenny was impatient.

"A what?"

"A solvent abuser. Once you're done, get round the shops. Oh, and here is a list of the stuff you should try to buy," Colin examined the list. He discovered the awful truth. Colin hadn't been listening when Kenny had addressed the whole newsroom, being too wrapped up in his own calamity and his prams. "Hang on! Hang on!" he squealed. "You're trying to finger people, aren't you – catch them out selling any of this?" Colin pointed at the list. He was getting very agitated.

"To an obvious glue sniffer, yeah," Kenny confirmed.

"These could be my customers," he wailed. "It wouldn't be ethical."

Kenny smiled at this. The idea of an ethical Colin did not come easily.

"Do I have to do this? I've got a reputation in this town."

Kenny was dismissive. "I know. That's why they'll believe you want the stuff. Now remember – if anyone sells to you, get right back to us here so that we can keep track."

"Except if they advertise with the paper?" he wheedled, not very hopefully.

Lynda, who had by now joined them, and Kenny chorused an emphatic "No!"

Colin flinched apologetically. "Just a thought. Can I help it if I'm a bleeding heart?" He was probably serious.

Colin caught sight of Julie approaching with her dreadful spotty make-up kit and the onion to make his eyes water. At least he knew now why so many of the news team were looking a little under par. The closeness to disaster focussed his mind. "I can do better," he shrieked, and fled from their clutches to the telephone. He shouted back for the names of some shops that hadn't been done yet.

It was a changed, not to say rapturous, Colin, who sidled back shortly after. "This is so beautiful! Kenny, it's so beautiful!" he eulogized.

"Why do I know he is talking about money?" Kenny asked nobody in particular.

Colin ignored the comment. "I'm calling these guys, right – the ones that don't know they're being hit? I'm saying, 'Hey, we're doing a big feature on your shop' – which is true – 'so why don't you take out an advert to beef up the impact?' And they're saying. 'Hey, great deal!' Then I'm stinging them for twice the normal rate because of the spread they're getting. It's beautiful! They're paying us to expose them."

"Colin, you are remembering it was our idea?" Lynda ventured.

Colin was not going to let pettiness spoil the perfection of the moment. "*Remembering*?" he said, magnanimously. "Hey, guys! I'd never have thought it up without you!" Colin drifted off again on his cloud towards the phone.

Kenny and Lynda shook their heads with a kind of grudging admiration. "Do you think we should tell him we're giving all the money to the local hospital?"

"Don't be cruel," Kenny replied, grinning.

They returned to the control board. Lynda picked up one of the rakes thoughtfully. She was still concerned about Roger's team. Scaring them wasn't the answer, Lynda decided. They were already going as fast as they could. She studied the board a bit longer, and then said, "Maybe Lisa's team could help them out. They're only two streets away." She pointed at the plan as she spoke. She'd give them their new instructions when they phoned in.

The campaign pushed on and in the hours that followed every likely shop in the town was visited. The board filled up with the direct hits showing up clearly. Julie suddenly appeared beside Kenny and Lynda. She had prepared the mock-up of the front page.

"What do you think?" The pair studied it carefully as Julie stood by for the verdict.

It was Kenny who broke the silence. "Well there it is, Lynda. The biggest front page we've ever done."

The headline screamed out at them. *THE SHOPS THAT SELL DEATH*. Lynda nodded. "We'll go with that." She knew as she said it that they were declaring war – total war, she thought, as she remembered Colin's contribution. A dirty fight lay ahead and she didn't care. Kenny too was pleased. He had done what he had to do. He wondered what Jenny would make of the "boy reporter" now.

But that was only a mock-up of a front page. The paper had still to be written, the whole special edition. It would take a team effort but the brunt of the writing would be borne by Lynda, Kenny and Sarah. It had to be good.

23.
SPECIAL EDITION

Even the printers, famed for their easy indifference to the content of the paper, raised a collective eyebrow as the Special Edition rolled off the presses. More than an eyebrow was raised in the town.

Under the huge headline, *SHOPS THAT SELL DEATH* which dominated the front page, appeared an uncompromising and sharply-written statement of the *Junior Gazette*'s opinion. Then followed page after page filled with photographs of local shops, each headlined with one word, *EXPOSED* and the name of the shop. Each was captioned with a brief, accurate description of what had happened when the *Gazette* team paid a call and obtained an illegal supply of solvent based products. It was devastating stuff and Lynda had never been so thorough on checking and rechecking the copy, making sure that all content was first-hand and positively vetted.

There could be no room for hearsay or guesswork or supposition. If it didn't measure up one hundred and fifty per cent, then it was out. Once before, in their very first edition, they had let their imaginations distort their judgment and it concerned the shopkeepers then too. Only luck and an appreciative Detective Inspector Hawkins at the local nick had saved them then. Lynda couldn't depend on it a second time. She had to know they were wind- and water-tight when the storm broke.

And break it did. Mainly on the telephone and usually anonymously. The nicer ones, according to Lynda, simply concentrated on her and the news team's characters, intelligence and doubtful parentage. Sometimes she managed to get them to give away their identity. That worked a treat – a renewed outburst and a swift and entirely predictable banging-down of the receiver. One particularly stupid caller gave away his identity and the fact that he had been selling solvents illegally despite the fact that he had been missed and hadn't appeared in the Paper!

Throughout the whole tiresome business Lynda stayed cool and polite. She reckoned that was pretty nasty!

Lynda was still on the phone when Kenny arrived back from his visit to see Inspector Hawkins. The Inspector had kept up his interest in the Paper's development ever since their nosedive on take-off. This latest feature was certainly very much in his territory.

Kenny listened to Lynda patiently, bringing another fan club phonecall to an end. "Yes, we can verify everything it says in the paper – and if anyone asks we will . . . Well, thank you very much, you're too kind. Please call again." Lynda replaced the receiver and said to Spike, "That's the fourth death threat today."

Spike, who had seen Kenny come in, turned to him and asked, "How did it go at the police station?"

Kenny nodded a greeting to the two of them. "Inspector Hawkins says he can't approve of what we're doing – and congratulations."

Lynda wanted to know if the Inspector was following it up, which was hardly surprising in view of the flak she was taking.

Kenny grinned. "Of course not – and he'll let us know when he has."

"Great!" Lynda was relieved. And she had her own good news for Kenny. "Kerr says it's the best edition we've produced and wants to speak to you personally."

"Yeah?" Kenny was a little disbelieving.

"Yeah, he wants to shake the hand of the person responsible. This story's the big one, Kenny! We'll be weeks just clearing up after it. So well done – and welcome back. Oh, and Kenny . . ." But Lynda changed her mind. "Never mind."

Kenny looked a little puzzled and headed off for his desk. Lynda turned to Spike. "Temporary Acting Assistant Editor!"

"Yeah!"

"You're fired!"

"Thanks, boss," Spike said eagerly. "You won't regret this!"

Since his return under a cloud Kenny had worked mainly out of his briefcase – the one he had got for the switch. He dumped it on his temporary desk and froze. There was an identical one there already.

"I'm touched," said a familiar voice from behind him. "No other guy has tried to close down a business for me."

Kenny swung round to see Jenny leaning against one of the other desks, watching him. "Well, if you can't put a few people out of business for a friend . . ." They smiled – and then the all-clicking, all-buzzing, Billy came rolling up between them.

"Happy endings are so predictable," he said. "I like the unexpected. You know – princess kisses frog and it's a girl! It *could* happen."

Kenny laughed. "As sure as frogs are princes," he said.

Jenny, her eyes on Kenny, said, "Some of them turn out not too bad."

"Shall we go for a walk?" Kenny suggested.

"Let's." Jenny started to move towards the door.

"Easy for you guys to say," Billy commented, but he was grinning.

They turned back towards him and he added for Jenny's benefit, "Don't let this wheelchair fool you, kid. I'm just leaving my body to science – in stages!" All three laughed and Kenny and Jenny strolled over to the door.

"This story's bringing in a ton of reaction, Jenny. I'm glad you've decided to come in and help."

"I'm glad you've told me that's what I've decided." Masterful or diffident, Kenny couldn't win. Jenny always took him on the blind side.

As they passed Lynda, she was still glued to the phone. She felt that was the appropriate expression! Jenny paused to eavesdrop and heard her say, "I'm sorry you feel that way, but frankly I think selling solvents to children is more irresponsible than anything we printed."

When Jenny caught up with Kenny, she said, "It's mad really, but I feel almost guilty. These people could lose their living."

Kenny said nothing until they had reached the newsroom doors, then he stopped and looked at her for a moment, intently. "These people are not making a living, Jenny," he said. "They're making a killing." They went out into the soft evening air of late summer.

24.

SUPPLY AND DEMAND

Lynda smiled as she looked round the now-empty newsroom. Julie's department had given full rein to their creative instincts. Over to her right Lynda could see, through a painted window, palm trees framing a tropical island in a tropical sea. To her left she could see the tumbling white water of a mountain stream amid green rolling hills under a blue sky, all through a window with painted red curtains. Tulips grew in profusion over the panelled walls of the waiting room and inside, a full bookcase and a deeply upholstered armchair brought a hint of comfort to the Spartan furniture on which no one would wish to wait too long! All around the newsroom, doors and shelves were edged in patterns of white and blue and white and red, and Danny's darkroom door was a midnight sky covered with stars.

She had just got to her feet and begun collecting her things ready to leave, when Kenny returned, having seen Jenny to the station.

"Still here, then?"

Lynda knew that already. "Yeah," she confirmed. "Jenny get her train all right?"

Kenny nodded. She had got it, but he wasn't too sure what was "all right" about it! He didn't go into that. Instead he beamed at Lynda. "Not bad?" he said.

"She's very nice," Lynda agreed.

"True, true – but it's not what I meant. Today . . . shops that sell death. The whole thing. I think we got away with it."

"More than 'got away with it', Kenny. That was something. Even 'the man' was pleased. Which reminds me, you've a date across the way. You know, when you get your hand shaken. Praise and all that kind of stuff. Mind if I tag along? Y'know, take notes. Pity Danny's gone. I've never seen this before. It's got to be worth the front page surely! Banner headlines – *KERR SAYS – NOT TOO BAD*."

They were almost helpless laughing at various possible headlines when they reached Matt Kerr's office – but pulling themselves together didn't prove at all difficult. Mr Kerr had that effect even from the other side of a closed door. They knocked, and responded to the immediate "Come!"

Matt Kerr looked up. "The man of the moment," he said. "You know, by any standards that was good journalism, Kenny – soundly researched, strongly written and with an active follow-up. Well done, young sir!" He had moved round from behind his desk and shook hands with

Kenny. Then he turned to Lynda, holding out his hand, "And you too, Madam Editor." She remembered his comment about the only ideas editors don't get credited with being the good ones! She appreciated the exception. Then he added, "Of course, these standards are your standards now!" He invited the pair to sit down as he returned to his desk.

This was new territory for Lynda. Criticism she could handle – praise, that could make you dizzy. No Councillor Amanda Swanson trying to close down the paper because they hadn't been good little boys and girls. No catastrophic failures as had happened when they had featured Sarah's cousin. None of the usual desperate need for salvage operations. It was heady stuff. But she needn't have worried too much. Matt Kerr's last comment had concluded the eulogy. Now it was down to business. "So, what now?" The question was direct and unsettling for two people still trying to enjoy the immediate past. "Remember, there's no such thing as yesterday in this business," he said, discouraging any backward glances.

Lynda gave a brief run-down on projects in the pipeline, particularly the ones which had been carried over to make way for 'the big one'. "And there's still the clearing up to do after Kenny's efforts," she concluded.

Matt Kerr nodded slowly, looking thoughtfully at one and then the other. "Are you sure it's just 'clearing up' that needs to be done?"

They looked puzzled, at him, at each other. What's coming now? was their unspoken chorus.

Matt Kerr went on to explain what he meant. They had cracked a mystery that should never have been a mystery except for the action of a powerful, selfish man, who used his wealth and influence to suppress the cause of a family tragedy for reasons of pride. The truth needed to be told and they had demonstrated the technical skill not only to solve the problem, but more importantly to recognize that there was one in the first place. And they had taken the lid off a dangerous racket in their town. But simple exposure was easy. The Press was too good at that. Too often they exposed things that didn't exist, he had added with a flash of irritation.

But the *Junior Gazette* had gone further. They had followed the story through and let the daylight into the whole business, pointing the finger just as Jenny had done, naming names. They had attempted to cut off the supply at its root.

Of course Lynda and Kenny knew all this, but as Matt Kerr defined what they had achieved another thought grew in their minds. He could have told them, but that wasn't his way.

It was Kenny who picked up the thread. "Are you saying we have to do something about the demand as well as the supply?"

"That we should talk kids out of using the stuff?" Lynda added.

"Well, I didn't say anything like that – but I'm glad you did!"

"Yeah, a campaign . . . posters, slogans, . . . a song . . ." Kenny was thinking aloud.

And Lynda too. "We'll need facts, y'know,

statistics about solvent abuse. There must be other Michael Eliots, already happened, going to happen . . .!"

Matt Kerr watched with interest. He allowed himself a brief moment of genuine satisfaction. He had certainly stopped the backward glances. "I don't know about you two," he said, "but I'm not staying here all night."

Kenny and Lynda took the hint. They said their "Good nights" and left the office still both talking at once – and not in the least tired. Matt Kerr watched them go. They had come a long way in a few months.

All on a Winter's Day by Lisa Taylor
Lucy and Hugh wake up suddenly one wintry morning to find everything's changed — their mother's disappeared, the house is different, and there are two ghostly children and their evil-looking aunt in the house. What has happened?

The Old Man on a Horse by Robert Westall
Tobias couldn't understand what was happening. His parents and little sister had gone to Stonehenge with the hippies, and his father was arrested. Then his mother disappeared. But while sheltering with his sister in a barn, he finds a statue of an old man on a horse, and Tobias and Greta find themselves transported to the time of the Civil War. . .

Look out for these forthcoming titles in the HAUNTING series:
The Rain Ghost by Garry Kilworth
The Haunting of Sophy Bartholomew by Elizabeth Lindsay

THE MALL

Six teenagers, all from different backgrounds, with one thing in common – they all want jobs at the new shopping Mall opening in Monk's Way. But working at the Mall brings rather more than most of them had bargained for . . .

Book 1: **Setting Up Shop**

Book 2: **Open for Business**
The new shopping Mall is opening soon, and the six teenagers who work there are already having problems. Ian is fired from his job at Harmony Records because of his dad's interference. Amanda's trying to fend of Mr Grozzi's advances at the restaurant. Jake's trying to hold down two jobs at once. And Simon's temper is threatening to cost him his job at the furniture store. Will life at the Mall prove too tough to handle?.

Look out for the next books in The Mall series:

Book 3: **Gangs, Ghosts and Gypsies**
Book 4: **Money Matters**